ROUSSEAU, BURKE, AND REVOLUTION IN FRANCE, 1791

REACTING TO THE PAST is an award-winning series of immersive role-playing games that actively engage students in their own learning. Students assume the roles of historical characters and practice critical thinking, primary source analysis, and argument, both written and spoken. Reacting games are flexible enough to be used across the curriculum, from first-year general education classes and discussion sections of lecture classes to capstone experiences, intersession courses, and honors programs.

Reacting to the Past was originally developed under the auspices of Barnard College and is sustained by the Reacting Consortium of colleges and universities. The Consortium hosts a regular series of conferences and events to support faculty and administrators.

Note to instructors: Before beginning the game you must download the Gamemaster's Materials, including an instructor's guide containing a detailed schedule of class sessions, role sheets for students, and handouts.

To download this essential resource, visit https://reactingconsortium.org/games, click on the page for this title, then click "Instructors Guide."

ROUSSEAU, BURKE, AND REVOLUTION IN FRANCE, 1791

SECOND EDITION

Jennifer Popiel and Mark C. Carnes

BARNARD

The University of North Carolina Press

Chapel Hill

The University of North Carolina Press has been a member of the
Green Press Initiative since 2003.

Cover illustration: Jean Baptist Lesueur, *The Planting of a Tree of
Liberty in Revolutionary France*, 1790–91. Wikimedia Commons.

ISBN 978-1-4696-7074-4 (pbk.: alk. paper)
ISBN 978-1-4696-7236-6 (e-book)

ABOUT THE AUTHORS

JENNIFER POPIEL is Associate Professor of History at Saint Louis University. She is the award-winning author of *Rousseau's Daughters: Domesticity, Education, and Autonomy in Modern France* as well as a Fulbright Research Scholar and past President of the Western Society for French History. She recently recorded *From Spinning Wheel to Steam and Steel: Understanding the Age of Industrialization* with Modern Scholar recorded books. As an intellectual historian of the eighteenth and nineteenth centuries, her research has explored women's history, childhood, education, and individuality in the modern world. Her current work examines French Catholics such as Rose Philippine Duchesne to investigate the intersection of vocation, spirituality, and public activism.

MARK C. CARNES is professor of history at Barnard College and creator of *Reacting to the Past*. He is the author of many books in American history and general editor of the 26-volume *American National Biography*, published by the ACLS and Oxford University Press.

CONTENTS

3. THE GAME

5. CORE TEXTS

ROUSSEAU, BURKE, AND REVOLUTION IN FRANCE, 1791

PART 1: **INTRODUCTION**

BRIEF OVERVIEW OF THE GAME

Paris in Revolution, 1791

It is July 1, 1791. France nears the second anniversary of the Fall of the Bastille and the end of unchecked power for the monarchy; the place is Paris, where the National Assembly debates the final draft of the constitution that will likely determine the new government of France. This game recreates the political dynamics of this pivotal moment, as contending factions within the National Assembly struggle to create a constitution that reflects their views and priorities. The Jacobins, radicals in the National Assembly, seek a republic; the conservatives want to ensure the continued influence of traditional institutions such as the king and the Catholic Church; and the Feuillants, in the middle, seek to combine elements of both in a constitutional monarchy. Leaders of the Paris crowd (each chosen by popular gatherings in each of the 48 "sections" of the city) articulate radical opinions from the galleries of the National Assembly—and sometimes in the streets of Paris, backed by tens of thousands of the poor of the city, the *sans-culottes*. Through it all, other delegates, uncommitted to any faction, try to determine what is best for France.

The main issues under discussion pertain to the contents of the new constitution: whether or not the state should nationalize the Catholic Church, grant the king the right to veto legislation, and enshrine specific rights, such as freedom of speech and the protection of private property. But while the game mobilizes political power—chiefly reflected in votes of the National Assembly—the revolution was essentially a struggle over ideas and texts. Political discourse was shaped by the ideas of the Enlightenment, the intellectual movement that celebrated reason and science and disparaged many traditional beliefs and practices. The Enlightenment in France included such diverse ideas as Descartes's celebration of reason, Voltaire's witty indictments of feudalism and superstition, and the advance of science, medicine, and the arts as synthesized in Diderot and d'Alembert's *Encyclopedia*. The central influences on the revolutionaries' political views were the dazzling ideas of Jean-Jacques Rousseau. In *The Social Contract* and *Émile*, both published in 1762, Rousseau maintained that if people could be freed from social constraints and prejudices, they could enter into selfless political unions that preserved everyone's freedom. But while Rousseau's ideas helped initiate the French Revolution, the tumult of 1789 prompted Edmund Burke, a brilliant Irish political theorist and member of the British Parliament, to write his *Reflections on the Revolution in France* (1790), one of the great political tracts of the modern world. In it, Burke argued that political institutions evolve slowly, in accordance with the needs and customs of particular peoples, and that the French revolutionaries had erred in trying to found a new government on abstract utopian concepts. Texts by Burke and

Enlightenment *philosophes* such as Rousseau must inform all papers and speeches, just as they would have informed the debates in the French National Assembly.

While the Assembly delegates are deliberating on a constitution, they are also addressing the problems of running France at a time when the usual machinery of government—dominated by a powerful king, his ministers, and provincial administrators—has broken down. Thus the National Assembly must also decide what to do about the collapse of the tax collection system and the escalating deficit, the slave rebellion in the sugar colony of Saint-Domingue (present-day Haiti), the opposition of the pope and many Catholic bishops and priests to the French Revolution, and the looming threat of war with Austria, Prussia, England, and other monarchies of Europe. All the while, tensions seethe as riots frequently erupt in the countryside and in the laboring sections of Paris.

The sessions of the National Assembly, presided over by the president, will likely encompass about 12 months, roughly from July 1, 1791, through the summer of 1792. Although students must adhere to their personal and factional victory objectives as outlined in their role sheets, they are free to do so as they wish; they do not need to "adhere" to history. In playing this game, students do not reenact the history of France after July 1, 1791: they make it.

PROLOGUE

A Night at the National Assembly

Again, your hands are fussing with your wig.

You can't help it. Five minutes ago, when you rose from your seat, walked down the long aisle, and joined the line to speak, you knew you could do it. You would address the National Assembly of France. But now, you stand behind Abbé Maury (ah-BAY more-REE), and there are only three speakers ahead of him. Your heart is beating fast. The room has become stiflingly hot.

The fingers of your left hand have discovered that some of the curls of your wig have been squashed. You must have sat on it last night, when you were at Antoine's. Do you look ridiculous? Will people think that you are putting on airs for wearing it? Will they dismiss you as inconsequential if you take it off? When you climb the steps to the stage, and then up to the podium, will everyone laugh at you, wig or no? Perhaps you should have remained in your seat. Two other speakers have crowded behind you. You could slip out of the line. No one would notice.

Except Robert, Marianne, and the rest of your friends. They would know. Last night, when everyone had gathered at Antoine's after the meeting of your political club and you announced your intention of addressing the Assembly, Robert snickered.

"You? Speak in the National Assembly? Hell, you haven't even been able to get Antoine to bring us another bottle!" Everyone laughed.

But their jibes were prompted by envy. At the club you had delivered a rousing speech and nearly everyone had applauded, even Robert. Marianne even stood and cheered. But that was last night. Now, as you scan the great hall that was once the royal equestrian academy, you seek their faces. The line of speakers edges forward and, without looking, you step on Maury's shoes.

"My apologies," you say.

He glances down. "It's nothing," he says with a wry smile. "After all, this place was built for the king's horses, not for the esteemed legislators of the French nation." Then he lifts his head and attends to the speaker.

You look down and are struck by the glossy black brilliance of Maury's shoes, one of which is now smudged. Then you notice the perfection of his dress: the fine black hosiery, tight against his calves; the black silk pants, fastened above the knees with black satin ribbons; a perfectly tailored black coat, with red-edged lapels highlighting his office as abbot of a rich monastery. Imagine: a cobbler's son, now become a leading figure of King Louis's court! You notice that his wig fits his head snugly, its shimmering white in sharp contrast to Maury's black attire. His is the image of perfection, while you feel shabby. You sternly remind yourself that what you say matters more than how you look when you say it. But you still feel a trickle of sweat down the back of your neck.

Your fingers, having squeezed under the wig, are scratching your head. You probably shouldn't have bought the one with horsehair netting. Again, you catch yourself: you must stop thinking about the wig. You force your hands to your sides and look again at Maury. His face is animated. He raises his hand and gestures imploringly to the president, Charles de Lameth (lah-MET), seated near the podium. Lameth, searching among his allies in the center, looks away from Maury. Then Lameth lifts his chin and directs his long, pointed nose at Buzot (boo-ZOH), the speaker, a Jacobin, who is attacking the king and the very idea of constitutional monarchy.

"The king has deceived us," Buzot calls out in a shrill voice. "He has deceived all of France, who once so adored him. Why would a king abandon his city, his nation, his people?"

"Because he's an imbecile!" someone shouts from the galleries.

"An idiot!" another calls out.

"A monster!"

"Certainly," Buzot, smiling, raises his hand to the galleries, "we must never again allow him to escape. Perhaps Lafayette" (la-fay-ett)—his upraised hand now points at the Commander of the National Guard—"will be more vigilant in the future."

"What?" A voice booms from the right. "Is the king a prisoner in his own kingdom?" Cazalès (KAH-zah-lez), the cavalry officer, has leaped to his feet. "Who would deprive the king of the liberty ensured by this constitution?"

"We will!" The center gallery erupts in shouts, and the section leaders of Paris and their followers are stomping and yelling. Some shout obscenities. Those standing beneath the center gallery hurry out of the way, lest the whole gallery collapse. The gallery to the left, not to be outdone, has begun singing the dance hall tune, "*Ah, ça Ira.*" ("Ah, it's happening! It's coming!") You know the current refrain: the enemies of France will be strung up on lampposts.

"Sit down, Cazalès, before Barnave [BAR-nawve] shoots you again!" someone calls out, and the left side of the Assembly convulses in laughter. Last year, Barnave, a leader of the Feuillants, wounded Cazalès in a duel. The bullet deflected off Cazalès's hat and grazed his head. Cazalès's wig, you have heard, has been designed to cover the scar, curls cascading below his ears.

Several conservative delegates on the right, standing, hurl insults at the Feuillants in the center.

Ignored at the podium, Buzot looks at Lameth, who shrugs. Buzot gathers his papers and hurries down the steps. Then Lameth gestures toward Hérault (AIR-ro), a nobleman turned fire-breathing Jacobin, who stomps up to the podium. His speech will be just what the crowd wants.

"The king has abdicated. In fleeing France, he has renounced the throne," Hérault asserts.

"He never left France!" from the right.

"And he's returned," another voice.

"No," declares Hérault. "He did not return. He was dragged back to Paris in shame. We all saw it. With his wife, the Austrian whore. They were planning to cross into the Austrian Netherlands, to join up with his brothers. And then he would lead an Austrian army back to Paris to crush the revolution."

Pandemonium in the galleries.

"That's a lie!" from the center.

"Is it?" Hérault shouts. "Or was the king lying when he declared his support for the constitution? Month after month, 'I believe in the constitution,' he said. Yet all the while he was conspiring with his brothers and the queen's brother—Leopold of Austria—to destroy the revolution. To destroy *us*."

"No! No!"

"We must face the truth," Hérault continues. "France has no king. The king can no longer command the ministries. Or the army or navy. Nor can he veto our legislation.

I say suspend the king. End the veto! The National Assembly must legislate so that the General Will[1] of all France can prevail."

"No," from the galleries. "Lawyers are not the General Will!"

"The people have made this Assembly so." With these words, Hérault thumps the podium with his fist and bounds down the stairs.

Another speaker ascends. Just two more. Your mouth is dry, with a sour taste from last night's wine. When you crawled into bed last night, your head buzzing from that last bottle, you were confident. But doubt nibbled at your sleep, and you awakened in the middle of the night with a start, heart racing. You realized that your last paragraph had a logical flaw. You got up, fumbling for matches and a candle, and jotted some notes and phrases. This morning, after dressing, you wrote it all down carefully. But now you wonder if the argument is fixed in your head. Perhaps you should read your speech aloud. Your right hand goes to your coat pocket, and you feel the bundle of papers inside. But you and Robert always sneered at the timid orators who stood at the podium, clinging to their speeches and peering down at their papers rather that staring forthrightly at those whom they sought to persuade. No, you will not read. You must change minds—and votes. You must grab hold of your audience!

"The king was abducted," Hyacinthe Muguet de Nanthou (Nan-two) declares. "General Bouillée has admitted it. Look at the letter. I have a copy here. It says: 'I arranged everything, decided everything, ordered everything. I alone gave the orders, not the king. It is against me alone that you should direct your bloody fury.' Don't you see? The king has done nothing wrong. He did not leave the country. He did not break any laws. He has committed no crime. He must remain head of state."

"No!" comes a shout from the Jacobins on the left.

And, a second later, the thunderous roar from the galleries. "No! No! No!"

"And furthermore," Nanthou shouts, "last year we voted to give the king immunity. Even if he did commit a crime, we could not charge him with it."

"Then relieve him of his duties! If he's no longer king, he can be charged! Suspend him!" More shouts.

"We have a lantern post outside," from the galleries. "Suspend him from that!"

"He'd snap it, he's so fat!"

---

1. The term "General Will" reflected Rousseau's particular use of the term, indicating an almost religious sense of collective virtue. Political philosophers in England, such as John Locke, conceived of the general will more in the sense of political consensus, what Rousseau termed "the will of all."

"Without a king"—Nanthou's whole body shakes as he shouts—"without a king, our vast empire will fall apart. You seek to destroy the nation and bring anarchy upon us!"

A man whom you recognize—Saint-Just (SAHN-joos), a rising star among the Jacobins, identifiable by his long, unruly brown hair—is running toward the podium, pushing past others. For an instant, you're confused. He cannot be a delegate—he is too young even to shave. In an instant he has elbowed you aside. Maury, alarmed, steps backwards and reaches into a coat. Does the abbot carry a weapon? Now Saint-Just mounts the podium. Lameth leans forward to bar the way, but Saint-Just pushes him aside.

"The king is false," Saint-Just declares. "He is a fugitive king. A brigand with a crown. He deserted his post so as to paralyze the government and deliver us up to the horrors of civil war and anarchy! You speak of the Constitution! He tears the Constitution to shreds. We have no Constitution anymore." Lameth, tugging at his elbow, pulls Saint-Just away.

The next person in line has disappeared. Perhaps you should slink away, too.

Now Maury is speaking. His is the deeply resonant voice of someone accustomed to officiating at a mass. "This king, like all kings, is not perfect," he intones. "Who among us is perfect? Yet our king remains sacred, to us—and to the nation."

"No, he is shit!" The left gallery is in tumult.

"Dog shit."

"Pig shit."

"You *sans-culottes* in the galleries," Maury bellows. "Silence!"

Now Lameth has joined Maury at the podium. He rings the bell and shouts for others to sit down. Then he steps forward, pushing Maury to the side.

"Our nation is in danger," Lameth declares. "A handful of radicals, along with traitorous journalists—these Machiavellians of consummate perversity—seek to destroy the Constitution. The Constitution! We must defend it to the death. I declare, as do all men of conscience in this Assembly: to King and Constitution."

Thunderous applause from the center, intermingled with jeers and shouts. Everyone is on their feet. Maury steps back from the podium, turns and makes his way down the stairs. Your eyes meet and he smiles: "And thus do the people govern themselves."

Lameth, at the podium, is ringing the bell and calling for order. Then he turns and gestures for you to come up.

Your wig is straight—you're patting it again. But now you draw yourself up. Looking carefully at the steps, you take a firm grip on the rail as you climb the stairs to the podium. Lameth moves away and his bell falls silent. As you look out at the sea of faces below, and at the galleries above, you feel dizzy.

You recall Robert's advice: "Speak slowly—that's the key." You take a deep breath, and wait for the noise to subside.

"Don't sway from side to side. The swayers look like monkeys," Marianne had advised. "Stand still!"

"Look at everyone—as if you want to seduce them all," Charles had suggested. "Just pretend you're a whore!"

Your hand reaches toward your wig, but you stop.

Then all becomes clear, a moment of crisp transcendence. It does not matter if your wig is straight or your words are perfect. You have something to say that needs to be said. France needs your passion, your honesty, and your ideas.

And so, with a strange thrill in your heart, you begin, your voice echoing in the great hall:

"Citizens!"

Note: This rendering of the emergency meetings of the National Assembly in late June 1791 is adapted from Timothy Tackett, *When the King Took Flight* (2003), and other sources. Some elements are fictional. The words attributed to Saint-Just were actually spoken by Marc-Guillaume Vadier, another Jacobin.

HOW TO REACT

Reacting to the Past is a series of historical role-playing games. After a few preparatory lectures, the game begins and the students are in charge. Set in moments of heightened historical tension, the games place students in the roles of historical figures. By reading the game book and their individual role sheets, students discover their objectives, potential allies, and the forces that stand between them and victory. They must then attempt to achieve victory through formal speeches, informal debate, negotiations, and (sometimes) conspiracy. Outcomes sometimes part from actual history; a postmortem session sets the record straight.

The following is an outline of what you will encounter in Reacting and what you will be expected to do.

Game Setup

Your instructor will spend some time before the beginning of the game helping you to understand the historical context for the game. During the setup period, you will use several different kinds of material:

- You have received the game book (from which you are reading now), which includes historical information, rules and elements of the game, and essential documents.

- Your instructor will provide you with a role sheet, which provides a short biography of the historical figure you will model in the game as well as that person's ideology, objectives, responsibilities, and resources. Your role may be an actual historical figure or a composite.

In addition to the game book, you may also be required to read historical documents or books written by historians. These provide additional information and arguments for use during the game.

Read all of this contextual material and all of these documents and sources before the game begins. And just as important, go back and reread these materials throughout the game. A second and third reading while *in role* will deepen your understanding and alter your perspective, for ideas take on a different aspect when seen through the eyes of a partisan actor.

Students who have carefully read the materials and who know the rules of the game will invariably do better than those who rely on general impressions and uncertain memories.

Game Play

Once the game begins, class sessions are presided over by students. In most cases, a single student serves as a kind of presiding officer. The instructor then becomes the Gamemaster (GM) and takes a seat in the back of the room. Though they do not lead the class sessions, GMs may do any of the following:

- Pass notes

- Announce important events (e.g. Austria is invading!). Some of these events are the result of student actions; others are instigated by the GM

- Redirect proceedings that have gone off track

The presiding officer is expected to observe basic standards of fairness, but as a fail-safe device, most Reacting to the Past games employ the "Podium Rule," which allows a student who has not been recognized to approach the podium and wait for a chance to speak. Once at the podium, the student has the floor and must be heard.

Role sheets contain private, secret information which students are expected to guard. You are advised, therefore, to exercise caution when discussing your role with others. Your role sheet probably identifies likely allies, but even they may not always be trustworthy. However, keeping your own counsel, or saying nothing to anyone, is not an option. In order to achieve your objectives, you *must* speak with others. You will never muster the voting strength to prevail without allies. Collaboration and coalition building are at the heart of every game.

These discussions must lead to action, which often means proposing, debating, and passing legislation. Someone therefore must be responsible for introducing the measure and explaining its particulars. And always remember that a Reacting game is only a game—resistance, attack, and betrayal are not to be taken personally, since game opponents are merely acting as their roles direct.

Some games feature strong alliances called *factions*: these are tight-knit groups with fixed objectives. Games with factions all include roles called Indeterminates, who operate outside of the established factions. Not all Indeterminates are entirely neutral; some are biased on certain issues. If you are in a faction, cultivating Indeterminates is in your interest, since they can be convinced to support your position. If you are lucky enough to have drawn the role of an Indeterminate you should be pleased; you will likely play a pivotal role in the outcome of the game.

Game Requirements

Students in Reacting practice persuasive writing, public speaking, critical thinking, teamwork, negotiation, problem solving, collaboration, adapting to changing circumstances, and working under pressure to meet deadlines. Your instructor will explain the specific requirements for your class. In general, though, a Reacting game asks you to perform three distinct activities:

Reading and Writing. This standard academic work is carried on more purposefully in a Reacting course, since what you read is put to immediate use, and what you write is meant to persuade others to act the way you want them to. The reading load may have slight variations from role to role; the writing requirement depends on your particular course. Papers are often policy statements, but they can also be autobiographies, battle plans, spy reports, newspapers, poems, or after-game reflections. Papers provide the foundation for the speeches delivered in class.

Public Speaking and Debate. In the course of a game, almost everyone is expected to deliver at least one formal speech from the podium (the length of the game and the size of the class will determine the number of speeches). Debate follows. It can be impromptu, raucous, and fast-paced, and results in decisions voted on by the body. Gamemasters may stipulate that students must deliver their papers from memory when at the podium, or may insist that students wean themselves from dependency on written notes as the game progresses.

Wherever the game imaginatively puts you, it will surely not put you in the classroom of a twenty-first-century American college. Accordingly, the colloquialisms and familiarities of today's college life are out of place. Never open your speech with a salutation like "Hi guys" when something like "Fellow citizens!" would be more appropriate.

Never be friendless when standing at the podium. Do your best to have at least one supporter second your proposal, come to your defense, or admonish inattentive members of the body. Note-passing and side conversations, while common occurrences, will likely spoil the effect of your speech; so you and your supporters should insist upon order before such behavior becomes too disruptive. Ask the presiding officer to assist you, if necessary, and the Gamemaster as a last resort.

Strategizing. Communication among students is an essential feature of Reacting games. You will find yourself writing emails, texting, attending out-of-class meetings, or gathering for meals on a fairly regular basis. The purpose of frequent communication is to lay out a strategy for advancing your agenda and thwarting the agenda of your opponents, and to hatch plots to ensnare individuals troubling to your cause. When communicating with a fellow student in or out of class, always assume that he or she is speaking to you in role. If you want to talk about the "real world," make that clear.

COUNTERFACTUALS FOR *ROUSSEAU, BURKE, AND REVOLUTION IN FRANCE, 1791*

No Legislative Assembly. In September, 1791, the National Constituent Assembly—referred to in your materials as the National Assembly —voted to dissolve itself and form a new body, the Legislative Assembly. By law, no member of the National Assembly was allowed to serve in the Legislative Assembly. This law, which would remove all of the players from the game, will NOT take effect. The National Assembly must remain throughout the game, although its function and composition can be altered.

Time Passes Swiftly. The game begins on July 1, 1791. But while your class may meet on Monday—and then again on Wednesday—far more time will have elapsed in your "France." Perhaps the time between each of your game sessions will amount to a month, or perhaps even two or three. You will never know for sure. The Gamemaster will provide some clues as to "where" the class is in real history by issuing Gamemaster News Service updates periodically. For example, if the Gamemaster News Service indicates that a ship as sailed into Rouen with word that Virginia ratified the Bill of Rights on December 15, 1791—then your game has likely moved into early 1792.

It is July 1, 1791. What happens in France after July 1, 1791 may be very different from what appears in the actual historical record. The players of the game may change history. Players may wish to research the historical background of other players in the game. But researchers must always remember that no player is bound to do what his or her historical figure did after July 1, 1791. You cannot say, for example, "Don't listen to Delegate X. He's planning to flee the country next month and I can prove it. Look at page 213 of this history." Delegate X may be making no such plans. Any historical evidence pertaining to figures in the game, and to French history after July 1, 1791, will probably be disallowed. But outside of France most historical events will likely occur as in history, regardless of what happens in your game. For example, the decisions of the French National Assembly would have little influence on the decision of American states to ratify the Constitution of the United States.

PART 2: **HISTORICAL BACKGROUND**

CHRONOLOGY

1787 to July 1, 1791

1787
- February 22: The First Assembly of Notables meets to discuss fiscal issues and rejects the possibility of increasing taxes.
- November 19: Edict of Toleration for Protestants is issued.

1788
- July–September: Poor harvests throughout the country.
- August 8: King Louis XVI calls the Estates General for May 1, 1789.

1789
- January: Abbé Sieyès publishes "What Is the Third Estate?"
- April 27–28: Réveillon riots erupt in the Saint-Antoine neighborhood of Paris over questions of pay, food, and unemployment. Troops from the French Guard arrive and suppress the riots by force.
- May 5: Estates General opens, but orders quickly deadlock on the issue of voting: large portions of the First and Second Estates support the idea of meeting as separate bodies, while members of the Third Estate remain adamant about asserting their numerical superiority and refuse to meet separately. The stalemate lasts for over a month.
- June 12–19: Sieyès forces the issue and Third Estate deputies begin to meet, but offer to admit deputies from the other Estates. They begin to call themselves the National Assembly, and the First Estate (clergy) votes to join them. Some "patriot" nobility join forces with them, too.
- June 20: National Assembly members arrive at their usual meeting spot to find it locked. They meet at a nearby tennis court. Under the leadership of Mounier and Bailly, they take the "Tennis Court Oath" not to disband until they have provided the nation with a constitution.
- June 27: The king accepts the creation of the National Assembly and orders the First and Second Estates to join it as a "Constituent Assembly."
- Early July: Unrest in Paris leads the king to call up approximately 20,000 Swiss and German mercenaries, whom he places at strategic locations from Paris to Versailles. This increases unrest, especially in Paris.
- July 11: Louis XVI dismisses Necker and appoints a new royalist, anti-reform ministry.

- July 12–14: News of these actions sends Paris into a fury. Crowds form and begin looking for munitions to protect themselves. The people focus their attack on the Hôtel des Invalides, where they find arms but no gunpowder or shot, and then, looking for gunpowder, focus on the Bastille, a famous symbol of tyranny. Many French Guard members join the side of the crowd and both locations fall. The governor of the Bastille, the Marquis de Launay, is killed by the crowd and his head is mounted on a pike, along with other officers of the Bastille garrison.
- July 16: The king again recalls Necker to the ministry as Director of General Finances and Minister of State.
- July 17: The king travels to Paris and is received by Bailly at the Hôtel de Ville, where he symbolically accepts the end of the Ancien Régime.
- July–August: The "Great Fear," a provincial uprising motivated both by fear of impending repression by the aristocracy and by hope of destroying Ancien Régime feudalism.
- August 4: Patriot nobles, in a response to both Revolutionary activism and the provincial uprisings, renounce many feudal privileges in an all-night session of the Assembly, leading to the abolition of feudal rights and preferential exemptions for the nobility, the clergy, the upper middle class, and the cities and provinces.
- August 11: The National Assembly formally decrees the feudal system abolished.
- August 26: The National Assembly adopts the *Declaration of the Rights of Man and of the Citizen*, a sweeping document that generalizes and summarizes the principles of the Revolution: rights, liberty, and sovereignty. The Assembly then turns its focus to drafting the constitution.
- September 10: The Constituent Assembly votes overwhelmingly against the formation of a bicameral legislature on the British Parliamentary model. The following day, the Constituent Assembly votes to grant the king a suspensive veto.
- September–October: The king avoids approving the August Decrees as well as the *Declaration of the Rights of Man and of the Citizen*. Foreign troops are again called up and placed in and around Paris and Versailles.
- September 12: Jean-Paul Marat begins publishing *L'ami du peuple*, a daily eight-page radical news pamphlet.
- October 5: Parisian women march to Versailles to demand bread for the city. They also insist that the king leave Versailles and govern in the main city, Paris. They are joined by men and, eventually, Lafayette's National Guard and some Assembly deputies. Meeting with a small delegation, the king agrees to provision the city and accept the August Decrees.

- October 6 (early morning): Some members of the crowd, angry at the queen, Marie Antoinette, break into the royal palace at Versailles, killing two guards. The royal family is forced back to Paris to live in the Tuileries palace. The Assembly relocates to Paris as well and exerts martial and social control to restore order and peace.
- November: The directors of the Caisse d'Escompte declare that they cannot approve any further loans to the state.
- November 2: The Constituent Assembly decrees confiscation of a large percentage of Church lands, with a total value of 2 to 3 billion *livres*. Anticipated revenue from the lands allows for the approval of new loans to the government.
- November 9: The Constituent Assembly meets in the Manège (the king's riding stables, near the Tuileries) for the first time.
- December 19: Nationalized lands are opened for sale; the Assembly issues treasury notes (*assignats*) backed by the state's new landholdings.

1790
- January 20: Joseph-Ignace Guillotin proposes to the Assembly the use of a machine for a more humane method of execution.
- February 4: King Louis addresses the Constituent Assembly and professes support for the Revolution's agenda, calling all French citizens to support it; deputies swear a civic oath.
- February 13: The Constituent Assembly votes to abolish monastic vows and to suppress, with some limited exceptions, religious orders. Some secular and religious functions are combined with the intent of making priests "officers of morality" and part of France's general population.
- February 26: France is divided into eighty-three departments.
- March 31: Maximilien de Robespierre is elected temporary president of the Paris Jacobin Club.
- April: The Constituent Assembly decrees that confiscated Church lands are national property.
- July 12: The Constituent Assembly adopts the Civil Constitution of the Clergy.
- July 14: The first anniversary of the fall of the Bastille is commemorated at the Champ de Mars during the Festival of the Federation. The king participates in the Festival and swears an oath to the (unfinished) constitution.
- August 5–31: The Nancy Mutiny erupts and is harshly put down by General François Bouillé, an action applauded by many deputies but soon derided by the crowd.
- September 4: Necker resigns.

- November: Edmund Burke publishes *Reflections on the Revolution in France*, one of the most powerfully received conservative and anti-revolutionary commentaries on events in France.
- November: The Constituent Assembly declares that Alsace is French, and that its people wish to be part of France. The declaration rejects the claims of German princes over the region; the Germans reject the French claims and offers of compensation for the territory.
- November 27: The Constituent Assembly decrees that all public officials and priests must swear an oath to the nation and the constitution.
- December: Holy Roman Emperor Leopold II writes to the French government protesting its Alsatian policy. He is ignored.
- December 26: The king accepts the Civil Oath of the Clergy.

1791
- January 3: The Constituent Assembly decrees that priests refusing to accept the Civil Oath of the Clergy will be banned from public ministry.
- February: Election of the first constitutional bishops.
- February 19: The king's royal aunts escape France.
- March 2: The Constituent Assembly abolishes guilds.
- March 10: Pope Pius VI condemns the Civil Constitution of the Clergy. This is reiterated in the promulgation of the encyclical *Charitas* on April 13.
- March 28: The Paris Commune orders the closing of the Paris Monarchist Club.
- April 18: The royal family is prevented from going to Saint-Cloud by a Paris crowd that includes National Guardsmen.
- May 7–15: Debate on colonial policy and the status of free minorities in the colonies begins. On the 15th, it is ruled that black inhabitants of French colonies born to free parents are entitled to civic equality with whites.
- May 15: Robespierre proposes that current members of the Constituent Assembly be prohibited from election to the succeeding legislature. Proposal passes [Note: Reacting adopts the counterfactual tenet that this did not occur].
- June 14: The Constituent Assembly passes the Le Chapelier Law, which prohibits workers' associations and strikes.
- June 20–25: The royal family is found to be missing from Paris and is discovered in Varennes, near the northeastern border of France; they are recognized, arrested, and returned to Paris.

VERSAILLES TO VARENNES: THE FRENCH REVOLUTION FROM THE ANCIEN RÉGIME TO JULY 1, 1791

Understanding the outbreak of revolution in 1789 requires some familiarity with the larger context of France at the end of the eighteenth century. After all, when revolutionaries first began to call this a "revolution," they meant it in the sense of coming full circle, of arriving back at the beginning. **Liberal** men influenced by the philosophy of their age, which we refer to as the Enlightenment, argued that monarchy had overreached itself and taken away a number of rights that were natural to men of property and status, rights that should be restored to them. It was only later, as the reform movement began to escalate, that the word "revolution" took on its current sense: of massive upheaval and social change. Only then did rights begin to be extended to recipients who had never been considered worthy of them before.

The French Revolution, initially moderate in its impulses, and influenced by philosophical ideas about representation, monarchy, and natural rights, quickly moved to much more radical conclusions. What caused the desire for limited political change—the extension of some specific rights to men of property and influence—to spiral into the Revolution as we know of it, with not only the fight to extend civil rights to all men but also the far more extreme use of guillotines and terror? The answer to that question is complicated, but in its most basic form, an economic crisis—with a government on the verge of bankruptcy and unable to raise new taxes—provoked intellectual discussions about the rights and liberty of individuals to be discussed in the context of real, often radical, reform.

On the eve of revolution in 1789, the government of France faced a significant financial crisis. While the national debt had been driven up by France's desire to help fund the United States' war for independence from Britain, the financial burden was substantial even before 1776 as a result of nearly nonstop battles for prestige and influence on the continent of Europe, dating back to the reign of Louis XIV, the Sun King. Louis had increased the size of the standing army, and maintaining this large military made it hard to balance the budget. By itself, this problem was not insurmountable; during this time both Britain and the Netherlands had greater debt burdens in proportion to their populations. However, France had an inadequate banking system and was therefore unable to easily service the national debt, which was short-term and privately held—doing so would have been a bit like financing government expenditures by credit card. In a different context,

Ancien Régime is a French term that means "old order." It refers to the political and social system that was in place in France before the Revolution of 1789. In the Ancien Régime, instead of the modern model of egalitarian citizenship, everyone was born into an organized hierarchy based on old models, and derived rights and social status from their position in the hierarchy as well as the location in which they lived. In this order, everyone was subject to the king of France, and society was divided into three Estates: clergy (First), nobility (Second), and commoners (Third).

Liberal, in the historical sense, refers to people who held a set of ideas, derived from Enlightenment thought, about liberties and rights. Generally speaking, they believed in freedom of speech, freedom of press, freedom of conscience, and, for some of them, economic rights such as the right to free enterprise. They had been influenced by eighteenth-century writers such as Montesquieu, Voltaire, and Rousseau, who advocated for liberty in all these spheres. Jean Jacques Rousseau's philosophical ideas are of particular importance in this game, insofar as they engage with questions about equality, social formation, and political organization. Many revolutionaries considered Rousseau's *Social Contract* a seminal work for its formulation of innovative ideas about liberty and the organization of society.

an increase in taxes might have put a dent in the expenses, but France's system of tax-collection was neither systematic nor uniform. It tended to tax those least able to pay rather than the wealthy and privileged, who often managed to find loopholes in the system.

Louis XVI attempted to make changes in the system of taxation, increasing the amount that the nobles would owe, but the elites resisted his efforts with appeals to philosophical ideas, now commonly circulating, about despotism and unbalanced monarchical power. Some offered to allow the king the power to tax, but they always insisted on power-sharing and a balance of power, not something that a king raised on theories of **divine right absolutism** was likely to consider reasonable. The fact that the king's wife, Marie Antoinette, was seen as a foreigner and a spendthrift, cruel and indifferent to popular misery, served to further undermine the prestige of the monarchy. If Louis was listening to Marie Antoinette, no wonder he did not truly understand his duties to the nation!

When bankers began to refuse to lend the government money in 1787, Louis XVI pled with the nobles to stop fighting him on the matter of taxes. He insisted that the state would have to declare bankruptcy if he were not allowed to proceed with his reforms, which included a uniform land tax and the creation of a state bank. Reforms, though not the ones Louis proposed,

were certainly something that interested Louis's audience, and they insisted that he call on the **Estates General**, which had not met since 1614 during the reign of Louis XIII, and use it to ask advice from the nation. The notables wanted this body to meet because they expected that the elites would be able to control the meeting and bend the agenda to suit their interests—taking a greater share not of the financial burden, but of governing power. The debt crisis was now linked to a political crisis, one in which the nobility hoped to tame the monarchy.

Added to the political crisis were a number of pressing social concerns. The harvest in the fall of 1788 had been exceedingly poor, and it was quickly followed by a season of flooding. As a result, bread prices rose astronomically in 1789, threatening starvation for the poor. This problem was exacerbated by a slump in textile production. France found it hard to compete with increasingly industrialized Britain in the manufacture of cotton and woolen goods, so thousands of workers found themselves unemployed, which meant they joined other populations who were hungry, angry, and idle.

It was in this context of social and political crisis that the educated middle class, asked to contribute suggestions for reform, believed that they might have a chance for political influence and the exercise of rights. The men of the bourgeoisie complained about the system of taxation, access to education, and political representation. Most of all, they vented their frustration at the illogic of continued

In this map, you will see the historic regions of France as well as France's closest neighbors.

privileges based on feudalism: the social system in which the Church and nobility (and often some towns or even provinces) received preferential treatment while commoners were obliged to serve. Feudalism had made sense when nobles fought to defend the nation, but now many nobles never provided service of any kind, and commoners, according to critics, were forced to labor anyway. Feudalism created an entire class of parasites and the commoners were tired of being hosts.

By the time most of the deputies had gathered in Versailles in response to Louis XVI's request for a meeting with the country's notables, they had begun to hope that being invited to advise the king signaled a new, more cooperative, era in governing. Certainly, they had reason to think of themselves as deserving of representation, given how much the philosophical underpinnings of absolutism had eroded between 1614 and 1789. *Philosophes*, following Locke, Montesquieu, and then Rousseau, debated the foundations of society and the origins of inequality between men, arguing forcefully for the notion of a social contract that gave men the right to protect their own interests. Additionally, Louis XVI had already sought information on the needs of his people by requesting *cahiers*, or books full of suggested reforms, from all the provinces; it seemed as if the door to political transformation was open.

The socially prominent men who had been elected, and especially those from the Third Estate (the order of commoners), were well-versed in rationalism, political theory, and the new science. They certainly planned to take advantage of this opportunity to advise the king in order to publicize their needs, streamline the state, and, ideally, increase their own power. In fact, as the more than one thousand deputies assembled, those from the Third Estate had particular reason to hope. For the first time ever, the elected deputies from each Estate were not equal in number. The Third Estate had twice the representation of either the First (clergy) or Second (nobility), in recognition of the fact that commoners constituted more than 95 percent of the population.

However, the opening of the Estates General demonstrated the limited nature of the reform agenda. The procession of deputies was a throwback to 1614, with men parading in by order, dressed in the symbols of their authority. Clerics wore rich vestments, embroidered in gold, while nobles carried swords and military regalia. The deputies from the Third Estate were placed at the end of the procession, dressed in sober black, and seated at the edges of the room—a physical demonstration of their inferiority and political insignificance. The king and his advisors gave speeches reminding everyone of the royal agenda of financial reform and pointedly ignored the constitutional questions, other than to affirm that voting would take place by order. That is, the First Estate (clergy), after voting among themselves, would cast one vote; the Second Estate (nobility) would cast another; and the Third Estate (everyone else) would cast a single vote. Together, the First Estate and the Second could prevail on any issue, two votes drowning out the hundreds of deputies of the Third!

The deputies of the Third Estate recognized both the insult and the blow to their quest for greater influence. A power struggle ensued, with deputies from the Third Estate refusing to verify their credentials separately from the other representatives in order to send a signal that they would not follow the royal agenda or be co-opted into tricameral (three-bodied) voting. Many deputies from the nobility and clergy remained opposed to the idea of voting in common, or at least sought to begin the process by meeting as three separate bodies. This caused a political stalemate. The Third Estate felt that it could not give way, and the other two orders were unwilling to follow the dictates of commoners.

The impasse lasted more than a month, but these discussions persuaded the more liberal members of the nobility and clergy—especially the clergy—to be more sympathetic to the Third Estate. Many saw the king's attempts to minimize the role of the Third Estate as an affirmation of outmoded notions of hierarchy—including divine right absolutism and seventeenth-century political theory. The sympathetic deputies, steeped in Enlightenment ideas, began to make common cause with the Third Estate.

On June 12, 1789, at the urging of the Abbé Sieyès, a cleric who was strongly and publically opposed to hierarchy and privilege, commoners began calling themselves the only true representatives of the French nation. They opened their deliberations to any nobles or clerics who might wish to join them, and soon, three priests from the First Estate were received with great rejoicing into the common meeting. Larger numbers of deputies from the First and Second Estates soon sought admission to the Third Estate's meetings, and the growing group began to call itself a "National Assembly." Here, the deputies followed the logic of Sieyès' powerful call in "What Is the Third Estate?" (see the Core Texts section, p. 108) and argued that the Third Estate was the most significant and most useful portion of the nation, declaring that the king had no right to dismiss them or to override their resolutions. On June 19, a majority of the First Estate clergy joined the National Assembly, making it clear that political momentum lay with the commons.

Louis XVI could not ignore these challenges to his authority. The National Assembly had already begun to decide constitutional questions by acting as if they were national representatives. The king was faced with the choice of either accepting this new arrangement or somehow breaking the National Assembly back into the Three Estates of ancient usage. Though Louis was unsure of what to do, the members of his court had no such hesitation. In particular, the king's youngest brother, the Count d'Artois, insisted that the king dismiss his liberal ministers, including Jacques Necker, the finance minister and adherent to Enlightenment principles. Necker had attempted a number of small reforms that had been blocked by nobles and had suggested that the Third Estate be given greater representation in the Estates General, in recognition of the size and influence of commoners across France. Artois and other members of the court, for whom Necker embodied

A **constitution** is a set of fundamental principles that determine the functioning of a state. In written form, a constitution describes the proper way to govern and thus outlines rights for citizens as well as limits on those who exercise power. When France's deputies set themselves the task of writing a constitution, they were not only attempting to describe the state of things but were making a revolutionary claim to their ability to limit the power of rulers.

the threat of reform, agitated for the installation of ministers who would reinforce hierarchy and the sovereign authority of the king.

When, on June 20, the deputies of the National Assembly found their meeting rooms locked, they were certain that the king had listened to his brother and resolved to end reforms by forcing the Third Estate into submission. Refusing to be intimidated, the deputies moved to a nearby tennis court, where, under the leadership of Jean Joseph Mounier, secretary of the Assembly, and Jean Sylvain Bailly, who had been elected president of the Assembly, the deputies took an oath not to disband until they had provided France with a **constitution**.

On June 23, Louis XVI assembled the deputies to make a pronouncement. In his speech, he reminded the representatives of the fiscal crisis and demanded that they pay attention to financial matters rather than focusing on government and social order. He emphasized feudal rights and the distinction between the orders. He also indicated that he was willing to give some contested political ground. The deputies, however, noted Necker's absence and believed it to be a sign that Louis had sent him away. Surely the king did not intend to reform, they reasoned, which meant that any concessions were minimal.

Lastly, Louis demanded that the deputies separate back into their individual Estates. Most nobles and a number of high clergy followed his command, but Bailly, in his capacity as president of the National Assembly, made the revolutionary statement that the Assembly was in session and could not adjourn. Honoré Mirabeau, a nobleman and a notable orator who had been elected as a representative to the Third Estate, refused to budge. "We shall not leave," he thundered at the guards. "Return to those who have sent you and tell them that we shall not stir from our places save at the point of the bayonet."[1] Louis, unwilling to disperse the deputies by force, gave orders to leave them be.

The Rebellion in Paris and the Fall of the Bastille

Upon hearing rumors of what had taken place at Versailles, the city of Paris erupted. The citizens took news of Necker's absence as proof that he had been fired and that Louis was opposed to reform. Parisians took to the streets to demand Necker's reinstatement. This tumult forced Louis's hand and he asked Necker, who had indeed resigned in protest, to return to the ministry. By the end of June, Louis accepted the inevitable and ordered all three Estates to meet as one body: the National Constituent Assembly (hereafter, the National Assembly). The distinction between the orders had vanished.

Of course, this was not particularly to the king's liking. Louis was hardly interested in accommodation except as a practical necessity. Conservative factions at court continued to work on the king, telling him that the best way to maintain his authority was to bring in troops and use force to dissolve the National Assembly. Aware that the professional French army (the French Guard) might balk at commands to move against the deputies, Louis ordered some 20,000 Swiss and German mercenaries (paid soldiers) to take strong positions in Paris and Versailles as well as along strategic routes between the two.

The Assembly decided to send a delegation to Louis in order to object to the stationing of troops. The king refused to listen. He told the Assembly that his forces would be used to quell disorder and that if the Assembly was concerned for its safety, it should consider meeting somewhere farther from Paris. Forward-thinking deputies believed that Louis was trying to move the reformers away from their more vociferous sources of support in Paris. The Marquis de Lafayette, the hero of the cause of American independence, proposed a draft *Declaration of Rights* (see the Core Texts section, p. 120) modeled on the American *Declaration of Independence,* by way of response. On July 11, Louis again fired and exiled Jacques Necker and formed a new ministry, one that was royalist, conservative, and clearly opposed to reform.

Paris erupted in opposition. On July 12, Camille Desmoulins, a hotheaded young journalist, jumped up on a table in the middle of the crowd at the Palais-Royal and gave them the news: Necker had been exiled! Troops had been called! Citizens should defend themselves from royalist aggression and foreign troops! A procession through the streets soon encountered German mercenaries at the Tuileries gardens. Desmoulins's predictions seemed to be coming true. Incensed, citizens looked for guns and gunpowder to defend themselves. The crowd grew larger, as workers and activists were joined by rebel members of the French Guard.

The Bastille was the primary target of the demonstrations for many reasons, not least of which was its reputation as an infamous state prison that held political opponents of the state. While nearly all of its cells were empty in July of 1789, the crowd had no way of knowing that. The Bastille was also the center for much police activity, and the crowd believed that it would therefore hold both guns and ammunition. The mob therefore had many reasons to target this location: supplies, symbolism, and security. Eventually the gates were opened, but not before someone had fired into the crowd, killing a number of the attackers. The commander and some of his officers were killed in retaliation for the lives lost. Soon the mob had cut off their heads, stuck them upon pikes, and paraded them through the city. They seized gunpowder stores and added to the arms that the crowd had already commandeered, including muskets from the government arsenal at the Invalides. The city continued to simmer, and one of the primary magistrates of Paris, seen as a royalist sympathizer, was massacred by the people.

Rather than allow the bloodshed to continue, Louis gave way. On July 15, the king told the Assembly that he would withdraw all mercenary troops. The Assembly, pleased, sent a deputation, with Bailly at its head, to the city of Paris to let them know that the crisis was over. In a move that was almost comical, the king again reinstated Jacques Necker as finance minister. Bailly became mayor of Paris

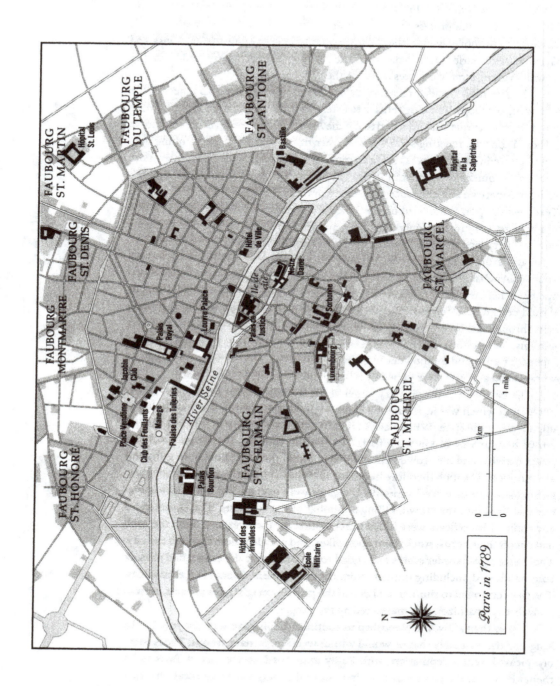

Paris in 1789

FAUBOURG ST. MARTIN

FAUBOURG DU TEMPLE

FAUBOURG ST. ANTOINE

Hôpital St. Louis

FAUBOURG ST. DENIS

FAUBOURG MONTMARTRE

Bastille

Hôpital de la Salpêtrière

Hôtel de Ville

FAUBOURG ST. MARCEL

Notre Dame

Île de la cité

Sorbonne

Palais de Justice

Louvre Palace

Palais Royal

Luxembourg

Jacobin Club

Place Vendôme

Club des Feuillants

Manege

Palaise des Tuileries

River Seine

FAUBOURG ST. MICHREL

FAUBOURG ST. GERMAIN

FAUBOURG ST. HONORÉ

Palais Bourbon

Hôtel des Invalides

École Militaire

N

1 mile

1 km

0

0

and the popular Marquis de Lafayette was chosen as the first commander of the Paris militia, now renamed the National Guard. Appalled by these concessions that placed reformers in authority, hard-line royalists, including the Count d'Artois, fled the country, where they could oppose the revolution more freely.

Louis had accommodated the revolution in Paris out of unwillingness to use troops in order to put down rebellion. Despite his capitulation, violence continued. Paris continued to be plagued by mobs and, worse yet, rumors of planned retaliation on the part of the nobles began to spread throughout the countryside. Peasants, already nearing starvation from two years of bad harvests, feared that an aristocratic plot would to return France to the conditions of the past, even as the deputies slowly began work on a new constitution. The departure of Artois and other nobles was seen as preparatory to their return at the head of an invading army of mercenaries.[2]

The Revolution Spreads

Other rumors soon surfaced as well, including stories of thieves and "brigands" coming to destroy crops or burn buildings. Peasants and rural villagers took action: they were eager to take advantage of new ideas about equality, to punish the excesses of the Ancien Régime, and to defend themselves through concerted actions. They attacked manor houses and chateaux and burned tax rolls, making sure that their individual debts were erased or that the records of seigneurs' special privileges would be destroyed. The provincial towns saw upheaval, too. Town artisans heard about Parisians taking to the streets and, like the peasants, rose up against the oppression of the Ancien Régime. While not every province saw this kind of uprising, the panic was widespread enough to be called the "Great Fear," and soon expanded in size, beginning shortly after the fall of the Bastille and continuing through August of 1789.

As the countryside erupted, the National Assembly continued its efforts to legislate for the nation. Its first mission was to produce a constitution, but it could hardly afford to ignore the pressing debt problem or the disorder spreading across France. In August, therefore, even as they discussed the *Declaration of the Rights of Man and of the Citizen*, the deputies also had to deal with the problem of the national debt. Necker, who would later propose the construction of a national bank, made it clear that further loans were necessary to keep France solvent. The Assembly approved these loans, as the only other alternative seemed to be immediate bankruptcy. The discussion demonstrated, however, that the primary issue for which the deputies had been called—raising new taxes—was taking a backseat to problems of reorganization and popular violence. This was despite the fact that the financial crisis continued unabated, with the government on the verge of bankruptcy.

On the evening of August 4, a committee that had been established to investigate the causes of the "Great Fear" presented both facts and rumors. They argued that much of what was occurring in the countryside bordered on outright terrorism, with manors being sacked and burned. They recommended that the provinces use force to put down attacks on landed estates and bourgeois merchants. In short, the committee wished to protect property rights by force.

However, a number of liberal nobles in the Assembly argued against this plan, claiming that force from the government would spark outright civil war. These nobles insisted that the attacks were a physical manifestation of the grievances of an oppressed people and, instead of relying on repression and military order, the Assembly should instead choose to abolish feudalism itself. More than one member of the nobility proposed not only an end to special fees and taxes, but also equal treatment before the law and the cessation of involuntary labor, all privileges of the Second Estate. To attack special taxes and obligations was to attack the philosophical underpinning of feudalism, and to insist that all men should have the same civil status. The elimination of other privileges followed, including provincial exemptions from taxes. Eventually, a number of parish clergy took the floor and offered to eliminate traditional fees for services. Soon other honors in the First Estate were abolished, such as the lucrative right to hold more than one church position or to tax the local population upon taking office. The question of Church reform was thus introduced. By the end of the session, which lasted for hours, most traditional forms of feudal privilege for the nobility, the clergy, the upper middle class, and the cities and provinces had been destroyed.

Not all nobility or clergy approved of the pace at which reform was proceeding; indeed, reorganization of the Catholic Church would prove to be one of the most vexing portions of the problem. From August 5 to August 11, the Assembly debated the particulars of the abolition of feudalism. Some clergy objected to ending the Church tithe, a tax that supported religious functions but could be onerous in practice. Deputy François Buzot replied, "First, I maintain that Church property belongs to the nation. . . The best course for the clergy is to save appearances by seeming to do of itself, as a sacrifice, what imperious circumstances actually force it to do."[3] Buzot's statement made it clear that, for many revolutionaries, there was little distinction between the Church and privilege. Conservative Catholic delegates dismissed such statements as wild-eyed radicalism that would destroy not only Catholicism but all of society. However, from the perspective of deputies like Buzot, feudalism was dead, and the Church, as a feudal institution, must be destroyed as well.

On August 11, the Assembly passed the August Decrees (see the Core Texts section, p. 117), formally ending feudalism. This ability to envision the abolition of privilege meant not only widespread reform of the Church, but also massive changes to other foundations of the system as it had been. In fact, August 11 necessitated widespread administrative reform.

Throughout the summer, both municipalities and provinces were reorganized in a way that replaced the complex divisions of the Ancien Régime and attempted to weaken local or regional loyalties. Eventually, eighty-three "departments," each about fifty-four miles square, would replace the traditional provinces (see the map on page 42). The process had also begun by which the old system of law courts, called parlements, would eventually be abolished. Parlements were not legislative bodies but rather judicial sites. Because laws and edicts did not become official until registered in court, these bodies had some power over a range of issues, including taxation. They were also the way in which nobility defended their superiority and privileges against not only the king but also the commoners. These courts and provincial meetings of the Estates were ultimately eradicated as insufficiently representative of the national will. This meant, effectively, that the worst abuses of the Ancien Régime had been abandoned. Unfortunately, the changes also had a negative effect: because taxation became nearly impossible in the short term, the fiscal crisis worsened.

Drafting a Constitution

Now that individual distinctions had been legally erased, all kinds of people— women, children, provincials, Parisians—claimed ownership of their nation. When the *Declaration of the Rights of Man and of the Citizen* (see the Core Texts section, p. 118) was adopted on August 26 as a prelude to further work on a constitution, the document seemed to further confirm these impressions. The *Declaration* offered sweeping generalizations about rights, liberty, and sovereignty. In language heavily influenced by Jean-Jacques Rousseau, such as the statement that "law is the expression of the General Will," the deputies offered citizens a concise summary of the principles of the Revolution. This document erased the Ancien Régime, put an end to hierarchy, and made a firm claim for individual rights. The nation seemed to offer such an inspiring and inclusive future to its citizens that some, hearing of the spreading financial crisis, donated their wealth to the government. Women sent gold and jewels to the National Assembly while men donated the silver buckles off their shoes to fill the coffers. Marguerite David, wife of the famous painter Jacques-Louis David, joined with other wives of painters in appearing before the Assembly where she offered her personal jewels for the nation, which was worth such a sacrifice!

The deputies themselves, however, had no unified vision for how these principles should be translated into a constitution. In fact, the Assembly debated in August about whether the declaration should be adopted before or after the constitution. A number of representatives, especially Clermont-Tonnerre and Lally-Tollendal, were concerned that adopting a declaration of universal rights before providing legislative specifics, including individual responsibilities, might mislead people, encouraging them to act much as they had during the Great Fear, without respect for property and propriety. In the end, however, a majority of voices argued that it was important to have a clear philosophical statement of the direction in which the Assembly intended to proceed. Thus the National Assembly adopted the declaration on August 26, as a prelude to the constitution and a clear statement of principles by which deputies might construct a new nation.

Agreement on general principles did not mean an end to legislative division. As the deputies debated the practical components of the constitution, they increasingly organized themselves into factions. Mounier, Jacques-Antoine Cazalès, and other representatives familiar with the English parliamentary system argued for a bicameral (two-bodied) legislature. In this, they had been influenced by Montesquieu's demand for a system with checks and balances. From their perspective, the position of the king, who would retain an absolute veto, would protect property and maintain stability. Property rights were of long-standing concern for many of the landed elite, including the rising middle class, all of whom relied on the money brought in by their estates to fund their lifestyles. As the revolutionary fervor spread, deputies on the right worried that some representatives, new to governing, might be subject to the pressure of the crowd and the "tyranny of the majority," and they hoped that a strong monarch would mitigate the strength of the masses.

Sieyès and Lafayette led the opposing charge for a unicameral legislature, which they saw as more representative of the people as a whole. They argued that strong monarchical powers would handicap the Revolution. After all, Louis had yet to actually approve the August Decrees and had made it known that he was dissatisfied with the radical direction of the Assembly. His continued references to the first two Estates reminded everyone that he still thought in hierarchical terms. Was this the person who would guarantee the rights of the people? As a follower of Rousseau's philosophy, Sieyès could not share Mounier's misgivings about popular activism. Did not the people know what was best for them? Was not the General Will always right? Camille Desmoulins's newspaper again popularized the debates, and as Desmoulins was decidedly on the side of the Left and the single house, he exposed those in Mounier's party to great ridicule, successfully painting his opponents as supporters of aristocracy and privilege. When the constitutional question arose on September 10, the National Assembly overwhelmingly voted against an English-style bicameral legislature.

However, the deputies were not yet willing to abandon monarchy, and the next day, the National Assembly defined the role of the king in the legislative system. Rather than an absolute veto, which was clearly out of the question, Louis was given a suspensive veto. This meant that the king could temporarily use his powers to keep a law from being enacted, but he could not postpone it forever, should the legislature continue to demand it. In practice, the suspensive veto, which took the action of two successive legislatures to override, was not significantly different than an absolute veto, but the difference was foundationally important to both the deputies and the population of the city of Paris.[4]

The Rebellion of the Market Women and the King's Return to Paris

The philosophical distinction was likely not lost on the king, either. He had resisted approving the August decrees for as long as possible and was now contemplating the meaning of his new legislative role. If he refused to sanction the *Declaration of the Rights of Man and of the Citizen*, would it cease to have power? If the king had been granted a veto by the constitution, could he veto the constitution itself? While Sieyès insisted that the constitution had created the king's position, and was therefore previous to his rule and required no approval by him, other legislators, especially those on the right, were not so certain.

The king, seeing the deputies in disagreement, resolved to act. He continued to stall on the constitutional question of approval for the *Declaration* and again called in foreign troops to strengthen his hand. Mercenaries again became a common sight on the streets of Paris and Versailles, and soon, stories about their behavior circulated that were even more sinister than in July. On October 1, the Assembly sent a deputation to the king, asking explicitly for his assent to the *Declaration of Rights*. That same evening, a banquet was given at Versailles to honor the king's bodyguards and the Flanders regiment, the mercenaries who had been brought in to protect the king and the court. As the story goes, the king and the queen both appeared at the dinner. The officers welcomed them with great emotion. As the couple circulated about the room, a song from Grétry's opera about Richard the Lionheart was sung, and the lyrics, which included the words, "O Richard! O my king! The Universe abandons you!" served as an emotional backdrop to pledges of support for Louis XVI. Officers in the National Guard, also present at the dinner, toasted the royal couple, took off their tricolor **cockades** and replaced them with white cockades, white for the Bourbons alone, without the red and blue that signified the Revolution and the city of Paris.

By the time the story got back to Paris, newspapers were reporting that the officers had denounced the Revolution and trampled the tricolor cockade underfoot. The city of Paris was alive with anxiety and certain that these were signs of a royalist plot to crush the Revolution by bringing hostile mercenaries to Paris. Revolutionary leaders called on citizens to march in self-defense. Georges Jacques Danton, a popular orator in the city, demanded that the militia be removed from the city, while radical journalist Jean-Paul Marat, known for his fierce tone, called for Louis to be brought back to Paris to live among the people. Parisians, both hungry and angry, found both Danton's and Marat's proposals appealing. They knew that the king's table would be well-supplied and believed that if he were brought back to Paris, their own access to bread would be assured. They were not sure if they could trust the king, but they also believed

A **cockade** is a circle made of ribbons, usually worn on a hat or lapel. Cockades were worn to indicate one's affiliation or loyalty, somewhat like a twenty-first-century awareness ribbon. Red, white, and blue cockades had come to represent the Revolution after the fall of the Bastille. Tearing off a revolutionary cockade—even without trampling it underfoot!—would be widely recognized as an anti-revolutionary statement.

that the court faction at Versailles was encouraging him to distance himself from the Revolution, and they wanted Louis where they could better influence him.

By October 5, a group of women, growing impatient at the inaction of the deputies and officials, decided to ask city authorities to do something about the scarcity of bread in Paris. The group grew as it travelled through the streets, with market women and men joining it along the route to the Hôtel de Ville (see the map on page 26.) Once there, the people demanded to see the officials and cried out, "Bread, bread, bread!" letting it be known that the source of their dissatisfaction was hunger, both their own and and that of their families. Some participants also indicated that they had heard the stories coming out of Versailles and were certain that the aristocrats meant to starve them out. While they had no luck in meeting with Bailly or Lafayette, Stanislas Maillard, a hero from the fall of Bastille, tried to persuade the group to leave the Hôtel de Ville and instead head to Versailles to see the king. Many were persuaded and left the city for the king's residence.

As they began to make their way the nearly thirteen miles to Versailles, both women and men joined the procession. Some were inspired by the call for bread, others by the desire for revenge, and still others were dragged along by the power of the crowd. The queen was a particular target of anger. The marchers claimed that Marie Antoinette was the source of the offensive banquet, and more than one woman was heard threatening to cut off her head and put it on a pike or to make a new kind of cockade, one that used her intestines for ribbons![5] Despite this, songs were sung in favor of the king, and the marchers claimed that they were going to liberate him from the bad advice of his ministers.

Once in Versailles, the women demanded bread and refreshment, which they were given, though they were forcibly kept out of the palace and the barracks for fear of what they might do to the foreign troops. The women began to search for shelter from the pouring rain and many of them, wet and tired, decided to join the proceedings of the Assembly as spectators. While from one perspective, the women's presence was a distraction, as the noise and crowding made it difficult to conduct business, some legislators saw their presence as an opportunity. After all, the deputies had been debating how to handle Louis's unwillingness to promulgate the August Decrees and to confirm the statements in the *Declaration of the Rights of Man and of the Citizen*. If the women were to be received by the king himself, then perhaps Mounier could be placed at the head of the women's deputation in order to present his demands alongside theirs.

A small selection of women were chosen to meet with Louis. They conveyed their demands to him, and he responded by agreeing to sanction the August Decrees. As in June after the Tennis Court Oath, Louis was a step behind the political tide and had agreed to a *fait accompli*, but the delegation was both pleased by his pronouncement and impressed by his gentleness and kindness toward them. Once Louis assured the women that he would make certain that shipments of grain were reaching Paris, they were content and left the meeting convinced that the king was indeed good, and on their side.

However, anger at the queen had not yet subsided in the group as a whole. Lafayette set a guard around the palace when he arrived close to midnight with members of the National Guard, but it was not enough to prevent disaster the following morning when an angry mob forced its way into the palace and toward the queen's apartments. At least two of the queen's bodyguards died trying to protect her, but the king, the queen, and the royal children all managed to make it safely to the king's bedroom. The crowd continued to scream for the queen's head, and it was up to Lafayette to use his considerable influence to calm them. He stepped out onto the king's balcony and then brought Louis, Marie Antoinette, and the crown prince before the masses. The crowd loudly cheered Louis and even greeted the queen with mild approval; this was a change of events for which she had Lafayette to thank. The crowd continued to clamor for the king to return with them to Paris. Some members of the National Guard, too, demanded the king's return. Thus the matter was settled. The royal family, accompanied by Lafayette's troops and some members of the Assembly, arrived in Paris late on the evening of October 6. The crowds that triumphantly accompanied them cheered that they had returned with "the baker, the baker's wife, and the little baker's boy" to restore prosperity to Paris.

The Attack on the Catholic Church

The Assembly relocated to Paris as well. The legislative body became subject to crowd rule in an immediate way, as the sessions were open to the public, influenced by spectators, and disrupted by noisy demonstrations outside the building. The deputies, like the royal family, became concerned about mob violence and anarchy. While the harvest of 1789 was good, helping with some of the most immediate concerns about food supply, the urban environment was still a pressure cooker. Not surprisingly, the Assembly made it a priority to pass reforms with the intent of alleviating the misery of the populace. For example, the *gabelle* (salt tax) was abolished, with the result that the price of salt, essential for making bread and preserving food, fell quickly and precipitously. The supply of foodstuffs to the city did seem to improve.

The Assembly also joined the king in suppressing unrest. Lafayette reminded the press of its obligation not to incite violence and radicalism, and the Assembly enabled authorities in Paris to declare martial law (signified by unfurling a large red flag) in order to assert physical authority over the city. The Assembly then tried to chart a moderate course. It debated voting qualifications and excluded most Frenchmen from eligibility by declaring them passive, not active, citizens by virtue of their failure to meet property qualifications. While all citizens were entitled to the same protection of the law, only active citizens could serve in the National

Guard. Equally significantly, only active citizens were entitled to political representation, with voting rights and, depending on their income, the right to serve as a representative of the nation. Desmoulins and Robespierre railed against this law and were joined by a number of the poorest French citizens from the activist districts, many of whom wished in vain to serve in the National Guard.

The Assembly, as much as it had any unified vision, was beginning to sense the depth of its power. If it could keep the masses in check, which two-tiered citizenship might achieve, it could use its popular support to chart a new course for the nation. However, the government had little regular revenue. It was one thing to repudiate all feudal obligations or to get rid of punitive taxes, but the government still owed money and needed income to pay troops and police, repair roads and canals, and otherwise provide the necessary services of the government. Matters came to a head when the directors of the Caisse d'Escompte, the closest thing France had to a national bank, refused to approve further loans to the state.

A suggestion by the Bishop of Autun, Charles Maurice de Talleyrand-Périgord, offered a possible source of funds: Church property. Buzot, a radical, had already implied in August that the legislative body, influenced by Enlightenment anti-clericalism, might look in this direction. However, Talleyrand's suggestion came at a particularly critical time. By late October, the government was in crisis; it had no capital to pay its debt and no way to move forward. The nationalization of Church lands would reassure bankers, because the land would serve as security for payment on the debt. Future loans could also be taken out, with the understanding that they would be paid back, with interest, as the lands were sold.

The debate over nationalization of Church lands centered on the issue of property rights, which were clearly protected in the *Declaration of the Rights of Man*. Did the Assembly have the right to confiscate Church property? Advocates of confiscation such as Talleyrand and Jean le Chapelier argued that the Church was a feudal institution and, worse yet, one that was deeply corrupt. If it had been given property in order to care for the spiritual and material health of the nation, then it only possessed that land in trust. Burdened by corruption and incompetence, the Church had failed in its obligations and had forfeited its right to control the land. Delegates in agreement with le Chapelier proposed that the Catholic clergy, as public servants, should be elected by and responsible to the general public, who would be responsible for paying them. For efficiency's sake, it would make more sense to confiscate the land and use that for bureaucratic needs, including church salaries, than it would to trust a failing institution to change its ways.

Not all deputies agreed. The Abbé Maury defended the Church and argued that property rights had been defined as inviolable by the *Declaration of the Rights of Man and of the Citizen*. Moreover, no single feudal "Church" owned the lands: hundreds of different churches, abbeys, monasteries, and other clerical bodies owned particular buildings and property. Was it not a violation of a natural right to take property from its owners without compensation? "We are attacked today . . . your turn will come," he warned.[6] Further, Maury and his supporters believed that confiscation would not actually solve the fiscal crisis. Once the land had been secularized and sold to private owners, from what source would the state pay salaries to the priests? Ultimately, confiscating property would not be more efficient but would leave the clergy without financial support or the ability to engage in active charity.

In the end, the opponents of the Church prevailed: secularization and confiscation carried the day, along with discussion of the rights of non-Catholics in the civil state. On November 2, the Assembly officially confiscated a large percentage of Church lands, with a total valuation of somewhere between two and three billion *livres*. With the guarantee of income from the sale of Church properties, new loans were quickly approved to keep the government solvent. The National Assembly soon authorized the admission of Protestants to civil and military offices as well.

The government could not sell off so much land so quickly, however, or land values would plummet, so it arrived at the solution of issuing *assignats*, or promissory notes, that were guaranteed with land. At least in its initial form, this was essentially a mortgage bond, secured by national lands, with the promise of interest to be paid on the loan and a state guarantee. Once the land was sold off and some assignats redeemed, others could be printed, especially if the value obtained for the land was higher than hoped. The men who stood to benefit most from these sales were wealthy men, including those in the Assembly. The Comte de Mirabeau, for example, bought up some of the first large blocks of land. This meant that the professionals in the Assembly had two reasons, beyond their philosophical opposition to the landed power of the Catholic Church, to see the nationalization of Church lands as a benefit. First, the sale of lands and the accompanying bonds allowed a nearly bankrupt state to remain solvent while it struggled with important constitutional questions. Second, the sale of Church lands opened up a new vista for the bourgeois aristocracy that was in the process of fomenting revolution. If indeed they had found their paths to advancement stifled—or at least slowed—in the years leading up to the Revolution, the sale of large tracts of land allowed them to become proprietors on a grand scale. On a smaller scale, any citizen who later purchased property that had once been confiscated would himself be supporting the Revolution.[7] Meanwhile, revolutionary politics continued to vacillate between promise and apprehension. The first *assignats* were issued, but, as the spring went on, investors demonstrated their reluctance to accept the notes, which led to a massive depreciation in their value and an inflation of prices.

Toward the Civil Constitution of the Clergy

On the positive side, Louis XVI addressed the Assembly on February 4, 1790, and offered his full support for the Revolution. His simple speech moved the legislators deeply, as he approved the reforms to date and offered provisional support for the legislators' work in producing a constitution. He also asked all French citizens to join him in supporting these changes, a rhetorical step that brought no less a man than journalist and politician Bertrand Barère to tears. The real question was whether or not Louis would stand by his words in the long term. Royalist agitators certainly remained unconvinced and continued to use their outlets, especially conservative newspapers such as *Les Actes des Apôtres* and *L'Ami du Roi*, to satirize their opponents and agitate against the Revolution.

In an attempt to ensure the fiscal credibility of the state and firmly underscore the fact that the Church was subordinate to the state, the Assembly voted to suppress both monasteries and monastic vows (see the Core Texts section, p. 125). The deputies argued that celibacy was not useful or productive. Priests were also assigned a number of secular functions in addition to their religious ones. For example, as "officers of morality," priests now had to proclaim and explain revolutionary laws from the pulpit. Initially, these changes met with mixed reviews; a large number of the lower clergy were persuaded to comply, however, when they considered the higher salaries that they might receive as employees of the state. Dioceses were subject to a national clerical map drawn by logic rather than tradition, which meant a reduction from 135 to 83 bishops. All of these bishops were to be elected locally, just like other public officials, rather than appointed from within the Church hierarchy. Though the ability to control and even sell the land was advantageous from an administrative point of view, the scope of the debts which the state assumed by taking on the Church obligations was also significant—on the order of more than one billion *livres* in debt.

In March of 1790, Pope Pius VI signaled his displeasure with France's actions and hinted that he planned to declare the French Catholic Church in schism— separated from the true Church and Christ's legitimate authorities on earth (i.e., the pope). Additionally, debates over the philosophical role that religion should play in society made clear the increasingly great divide between the beliefs of the philosophical and anti-clerical deputies and those of the majority of French citizens. From spring into summer of 1790, discussions became increasingly divisive, with clergy like Juigné, the Archbishop of Paris, asking for the Assembly to reverse course or at least seek guidance from the papacy, while others continued to insist that there was no reason for the Assembly to ask permission from the pope. Departments with a history of denominational conflict such as Alsace, the Midi, and Nîmes witnessed riots between Catholics and Protestants. Determined to underline their legislative commitment to religious change, the Assembly did not back down but instead, in July, adopted these changes in a single document: the Civil Constitution of the Clergy (see the Core Texts section, p. 128).

The Civil Constitution intended to reform the Church along the lines of Enlightenment thought about usefulness, tolerance, citizenship, and clerical abuse. Deputies who endorsed the Civil Constitution believed that they were not interfering with Church dogma but only reforming the civic aspects of Church functions. However, the Civil Constitution effectively nationalized the Catholic Church, denying both its hierarchical traditions and the ultimate authority of the pope in Rome. Many Catholic clergy felt that the Civil Constitution obliged them to affirm the sovereignty of the nation over their religious beliefs. A majority of deputies continued to insist on the nationalization of the French Catholic Church, in large part because the legislators tended to believe strongly in Enlightenment ideas that advocated the subordination of the church, as a public institution, to the state. The law demonstrated this emphasis when it required clergy to swear a vow of loyalty to the nation. The end result, however, was that clergy were required to swear a more forceful oath to the nation than to God, a situation that forced "a quarrel with a patriotic priesthood, and even [with] the religious feeling of a patriot nation."[8]

While Louis would eventually accept the Civil Constitution at the end of 1791, again as a *fait accompli*, nearly all sitting bishops refused to swear the oath. As Pope Pius VI's encyclical *Charitas* (see the Core Texts section, p. 133) became more widely known throughout France, parish priests and other clerics increasingly refused to take or even retracted their oaths, often with wide support from their dioceses. Outside of Enlightenment salons and legislative halls, many citizens began to feel that the Revolution was waging war not against privilege but against religious belief. Disagreement about the role of Catholicism in the life of citizens began to divide a nation that had, until that point, offered reasonably broad-based support to the Revolution.[9]

Perhaps the deputies might be forgiven for having prioritized their own, more secular, beliefs and misunderstood the wide support held by the Catholic Church. Taking the pulse of the nation was really quite difficult, due to an excess of information and numerous competing perspectives. From the time of the calling of the Estates General, multiple periodicals had sprung up to answer the demand for news, and both counterrevolutionaries and revolutionaries alike found an audience in popular journals. People of all political stripes clamored to be heard, and a range of visions existed among the revolutionary ones. Given the chaos produced by demonstrations, rumors, and the popular press, the deputies' reliance on an elite understanding of some aspects of the situation is understandable.

A similar situation prevailed in the royal household as well. Though the king had appeared before the Assembly to lend his support to the Revolution and had officially accepted the Civil Constitution, his personal feelings on the subject were less clear. Living in Paris had made him subject to the opinions of deputies, legislators, and crowds in a rather immediate sense. Accustomed to operating at a remove from public pressure, Louis was unsure of how to navigate this situation, and he turned to Mirabeau and Lafayette, also elite in their own ways, for advice and direction. Mirabeau was a particularly unlikely confidante, given that he had begun the Revolution by using his thundering oratory in defense of the rights of the Third Estate. In June of 1789, his ringing voice had strengthened the resolve of the deputies not to be dismissed and had forced Louis to accept the Tennis Court Oath as a practical matter. However, over the course of the next year, Mirabeau had become increasingly useful to the king. By May of 1790, Louis was paying Mirabeau to work as his agent within the Assembly, promoting the idea of a strong constitutional monarchy. On the advice of Lafayette and Mirabeau, Louis tried to publicly reconcile himself to his people. The king spoke positively of the Revolution as evidenced by the works of the legislators, including the Civil Constitution and the forthcoming constitution.

On July 14, 1790, Louis appeared at the Festival of the Federation, the anniversary celebration of the storming of the Bastille, held at the Champ de Mars in Paris. At this festival, the National Guard took an oath of fidelity to Lafayette, the law, and the king. Delegations appeared from each of the eighty-three departments of France. This was an opportunity for Louis to make a personal appeal to his people, and the periodical press made sure that citizens across France had access to accounts of the event. As individuals swore an oath to the nation, Louis swore to uphold the (still-unfinished) constitution. Some politicians claimed that the king's demeanor—sitting uncomfortably in an armchair and looking alternately bored and displeased with the proceedings—gave some indication of his true feelings. Despite this, the people cheered the king and the event was a rousing success, with urban artisans and elite attorneys, people from Paris and the provinces, all mingling and celebrating the first year of revolutionary change.

Representation, Authority, and Monarchial Control

In retrospect, however, Louis XVI and a revolutionary understanding of authority seemed set on a collision course. Paris hoped for a king who would embrace change, but the monarch's behavior seemed, at best, to represent a tense and minimal acceptance of the new political agenda. Many deputies distrusted the monarchy in general and Louis in particular. Legislative plans therefore opposed giving much real power to anyone outside the Assembly; the deputies decided against a bicameral legislature similar to that found in Britain, where a House of Lords might act in the interest of tradition or privilege.

Still more political problems loomed on the horizon. The legislators were not only battling absolutism and noble privilege at the top; they were also determined to restrict political participation at lower levels. The deputies had eliminated more than one-third of adult males from all forms of voting and all but the wealthiest citizens from standing as candidates. When they considered questions of race, as in debates over Saint-Domingue, an immensely profitable slave colony, their initial impulses were to leave voting qualifications in the hands of the white colonists (although this decision would be contested).

The legislative privileging of elite white men did not mean that political influence was entirely inaccessible or one-way. Through journals, political clubs, and public gatherings, members of the public, often urban and poor, could closely follow events, comment on them, and influence them through their participation in the galleries. Political clubs, popular societies that met to discuss politics, legislation, and social change, were not only for the elites. While the "Friends of the Constitution," later called the Jacobin Club, initially held meetings composed of deputies to the Assembly and philosophers (see the Core Texts section, p. 123), other clubs were far more open. For example, the Cordeliers Club allowed people of middling backgrounds and even women to participate. In some sense, the Cordeliers were the equivalent of a salon for radicals—messy, loud, diverse, and politically engaged rather than witty, sophisticated, elite, and philosophical. Many radicals were frequent participants in debates there, and public pressure coming out of this society was no small factor in the decision on June 19 to eliminate noble titles and status once and for all.

In practice, this meant that the deputies, the bulk of whom were moderate, likely felt embattled on both sides. On the right, there was a monarch jealous of his privileges, only halfheartedly willing to join the Revolution. On the left, there were ever more radical and public agitators: journalists such as Marat, Desmoulins, and others who believed that the distinction between passive and active citizen should be entirely effaced. These men wanted political equality and economic reform. This radicalism was not always even limited to white men. Clubs such as the Society of the Friends of Blacks, led by Brissot, addressed the Assembly and also distributed antislavery literature throughout France. Race was not the only contested category; social distinctions based on gender also came under attack. The Society of the Friends of Truth admitted women to its ranks and had such diverse male participants as Gracchus Babeuf, Barère, and Condorcet. Social barriers had begun to fall in all areas, or at least needed justification to remain.

As radical egalitarianism spread, it led to a breakdown in order. In August of 1790, the city of Nancy, near the border, saw a soldiers' revolt break into open mutiny as the rank and file were influenced by democratic ideas. Lafayette's cousin, General Bouillé, a staunch royalist, brutally suppressed the revolt on the Assembly's orders. The moderate deputies of the Assembly were grateful to see order restored, but very soon people of radical leaning, including those from the streets and the Cordeliers, condemned Bouillé's actions, seeing them not as heroic but as part and parcel of a history of aristocratic despotism. Public outrage at Bouillé grew. Denunciations of armed tyranny became a popular refrain, further discrediting royalists or those attached to them, including both Mirabeau and Lafayette. Republican sentiment expanded and conservatives increasingly began to flee. Even Necker, once so popular, resigned and fled to Switzerland in September of 1790. If Necker, the minister of reform, was not liberal enough, what of Louis XVI?

The radical left had found the power of its voice, in particular through the popular societies and activist journalism. Yet the deputies at the center of the Assembly were still very moderate reformers, committed to a limited constitutional monarchy. On the right, resistance to the Civil Constitution increased throughout the summer of 1790, and devout Catholics in the countryside bristled at the National Assembly's "interference" in the affairs of the Church. Throughout it all, payment of the government's debts and questions of economic stability continued to plague the country, with no easy solution in sight.

Additionally, concerns mounted about the king in an international context. Did Louis, like his brother, the Count d'Artois, hope to use foreign armies to restore his own position? Or were his directions to the French armies along the border intended to defend the state? Debates over contested regions, especially ones where feudal rights were held by non-French nobles, such as Alsace or Avignon, made it clear that international diplomacy could not be unaffected by or uninterested in French domestic politics. Even if German princes or the papacy were offered financial compensation for the loss of their territory, that was hardly likely to be satisfactory. Further, the annexation of territories, with the claim that they wished to join France, posed a serious diplomatic question: did France have the right to seize territory that was in rebellion against its monarch? The Revolution asserted that it did, but that was not a situation that foreign heads of state would likely be content to let stand, which meant that their interference was to be feared, especially if Louis were to officially appeal for their help in checking the advance of the Revolution.

There is plenty of blame to be assigned in the inability of the deputies and the king to find common ground. On the part of the monarch, the most significant portion might be given to his religious devotion. Louis XVI was not an energetic or imaginative monarch, but he took his responsibilities toward the Catholic Church quite seriously. He had attempted to avoid approving the Civil Constitution of the Clergy for weeks while he sought guidance on the law. Two mutually conflicting facts seemed true to him: first, that the pope considered approval of the document to be equivalent to a schism, and second, that pragmatically, Louis could no longer delay approval without serious political repercussions from the radical factions of the Revolution. Since Louis, a pious man, could not in good conscience accept this document, he seems to have considered himself freed from remorse about double-dealing once he was compelled to approve the Civil Constitution in December of 1790. When Pope Pius VI officially condemned the Civil Constitution of the Clergy in April of 1791 (see the Core Texts section, p. 133), the stage was set for an open break between Louis and the Revolution.

As for the deputies, they recognized that the king was a reluctant revolutionary. However, given the increasing political and social radicalism of revolutionaries outside of the Assembly, and the dynamism of the moment, legislators hoped that the monarchy could still serve as a pillar of stability. The constitution that was in progress claimed that the king's person was inviolable and sacred, which meant that the monarch's very existence was a powerful symbol, and if he could be persuaded to act for the good of the nation, it could, perhaps, stave off further radicalization. In effect, they did not trust the king but were not ready to abandon the idea of monarchy—it was their counterweight to radicalism and street activism.

The king felt the weight of these tensions as much as the deputies. In the spring of 1791, the royal family resolved to test whether or not the crowd held them prisoner in Paris. The law allowed them to travel, but it was less clear whether the people of Paris would let the king leave the city. When Louis let it be known that he intended to travel outside of Paris on Easter Sunday, in order to hear Mass said by a priest who had not sworn the oath of loyalty to the nation, he received a decisive answer to his question. The palace of the Tuileries, where he and his family were living, was mobbed by people determined to keep him in the city. When the carriages were made ready, the group refused to let the carriage leave. Rumors said that if the king left, "civil war was to commence, revolutionary leaders to be punished, and the Revolution itself cruelly crushed."[10] Bailly pled with the crowd to allow Louis to go, as the law permitted, to no avail. The royal family sat in the carriages for hours and then returned to the palace, humiliated by what had transpired.

This event seems to have settled the king's mind once and for all about the wisdom of remaining in the city, directly subject to the whims of the Paris crowd. On the night of June 20, the king's younger brother, the Count de Provence, fled Paris. The king and queen and their children left at the same time, though not in the same carriage. Marie Antoinette and Louis travelled until they reached Varennes, on the far northeastern edge of France, at which point the king descended from the carriage and was recognized by a postmaster. He was than placed under arrest and held until troops arrived to take him back to Paris.

The city of Paris had heard of the king's flight within hours and immediately blamed Bailly, Lafayette, and the deputies for not doing more to prevent his escape. Crowds of citizens, worried about an invasion of France, thronged the streets. The National Assembly took measures to reassure the people and claim its power, but what appeared to be a betrayal by the monarch was a shock, invested as they were in shaping a constitution that relied on him. The legislators did not lose their political nerve, but instead prepared to defend the nation and let it be known that Louis had not left of his own accord, but that he and his family had been abducted and that they would relieve him of duties until they could discover what had actually happened.

Not all deputies were sanguine about this approach; some radicals wanted to depose the king and declare a republic then and there! The legislators who visited the Jacobin Club to discuss reforms nearly came to blows over what approach to take and emerged from the discussion so divided that a new political constellation

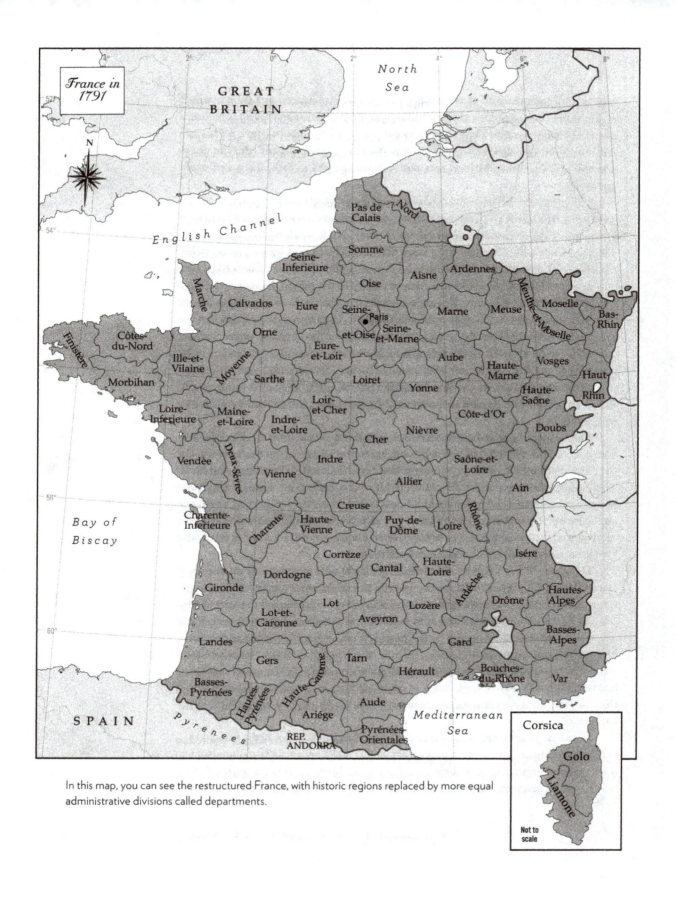

In this map, you can see the restructured France, with historic regions replaced by more equal administrative divisions called departments.

was born. Most deputies left and founded a new, more conservative, club, the Feuillants, which was now much greater in number than the Jacobins of Paris and deeply committed to constitutional principles and a peaceful solution to the crisis. The Jacobins, however, had the power of their outrage at what they were certain was the king's betrayal. They also had popular support from the radical Left.

When, four days after the initial flight, the carriage that contained the royal family returned to the city, the immense crowd that greeted them was eerily silent, neither hissing and jeering nor cheering, but reproaching them for their behavior with stony faces. The silence belied the turmoil of the situation, which was desperately uncertain. Would there be war with foreign powers? Could the king be brought to an understanding of his duties? How would the nation truly become united? Louis was once again in the Tuileries, but his fate, and that of France, remained to be seen.

FRANCE IN A GLOBAL CONTEXT: JULY 1, 1791

War looms on the horizon. This is nothing new. Until the French Revolution, most of Europe was ruled by monarchs and, though many of the monarchs were related by marriage, their nations were often at war with each other. Nearly always, the issue was land, the main source of wealth and power. Russia, Prussia, Sweden, and Austria contended for control of Poland, the Baltic, and much of eastern Europe; France, Austria, England, and Spain vied for the lowlands (what is now the Netherlands and Belgium); German princes fought with each other, and with France and Prussia, for patches of land along much of the north European plain from the Rhine to the Baltic. The Hapsburgs struggled to maintain their grip on their vast, polyglot empire, as the Muslim Turks nibbled away at the Austrian domains in the Balkans. By the 1750s the struggle between England and France had turned into a global war that raged from the Americas to India. Though the French lost the war—and with it, nearly all of North America and most of India—King Louis XVI got some measure of revenge by intervening in the American Revolution, assisting the upstart patriots in their war for independence. Eighteenth-century monarchs spent much of their time—and money—fighting wars or preparing for them.

What is new about this impending war is that France is no longer obviously the most powerful player in the middle of these power struggles, nor is her relationship to the other monarchies clear. The revolution in France in 1789 has changed everything. France, long the dominant force in continental Europe, has lost much of its military might. Louis XVI's officials can no longer collect taxes; the French army and navy struggle to keep the armed forces in a state of readiness. Traditionally all of the officers were noblemen, but since the fall of the Bastille, about half of the officers have fled from the army and navy—and even from France. Hundreds have joined émigrés under the leadership of the French king's brothers in Coblenz, a German principality in the Rhineland near the border with France. The king's younger brothers make no secret of their plans to invade France and overthrow the revolutionaries.

Other European monarchs, too, seek to exploit France's military weakness. Many German and Austrian noblemen who owned land within France are outraged that the National Assembly has repudiated feudalism and freed peasants of feudal dues. German and Austrian princes, too, covet Alsace and Lorraine, which French kings "stole" from them decades or centuries earlier. Leopold II of Austria may regard France's weakness as an opportunity to strengthen his control of the Austrian Netherlands. And Britain, intent on securing its worldwide empire, is, at least initially, reassured that the French monarch has been weakened.

But by the summer of 1791, many European monarchs have begun to reassess the situation. Will the revolutionary fervor spread to their own states? And though the monarchs might have been pleased to see their French rivals embarrassed and weakened, all monarchs are unsettled by the fact that Louis XVI and his family have become virtual prisoners in the Tuileries Palace in Paris. A rising tide of revolution might drown all of the monarchs of Europe. Rumors spread, too, that the revolutionaries intend to carry the revolution abroad, first liberating the lowlands from Austrian control, then driving the émigrés from Coblenz and other German principalities, and finally promoting republicanism everywhere in Europe.

In recent months, the crowned heads of Europe have begun to respond to the crisis in their own ways. Leopold II, after seizing Belgrade from the Turks, has given it back as the price of ending Austria's war with the Ottoman Empire. Austria and Prussia have resolved their disputes over contested borderlands in Slovenia and the Balkans. And Prussia and Russia have put their differences aside in their quarrel over Poland. The monarchs of Europe, including Gustavus III of Sweden, are closely scrutinizing the situation in France.

Many questions remain. Will the French army and navy fight effectively? A major question concerns the issue of command. While the king commands the professional armed forces, the National Assembly controls the funds on which the army and navy depend. The defection of so many noblemen has deprived the French army of half of its officer corps; many of the new officers, appointed by the National Assembly, emphatically endorse the revolution and its objectives. Moreover, some 20,000 taxpaying citizens have volunteered to serve in the National Guard of Paris, commanded by Lafayette. Tens of thousands more have volunteered to serve on the National Guards of their cities. Leaders of the sections of Paris insist that their followers—who seized the Bastille from professional soldiers—would willingly sacrifice themselves as soldiers on behalf of the General Will of the nation. In the event of war—offensive or defensive—these volunteer troops could supplement the mercenaries within the French army. In short, the military situation within France—and Europe overall—is uncertain.

Across the Atlantic Ocean, in the Caribbean, the situation is no more fixed. Historically, Saint-Domingue, the French colony on the western side of the Caribbean island of Hispaniola, has been the most profitable colony in the world. Though when Christopher Columbus landed on Hispaniola in 1492 the island was peopled by perhaps a half million Taino natives, their numbers dwindled over the next two centuries, many of the natives dying from disease and exploitation by Spanish miners and ranchers; eventually the native peoples were all but wiped out. In 1697 a French officer brought the colony under French military protection. At that point the island's population was only 10,000; half were white and the other half were black slaves, most of whom cultivated tobacco, indigo, and sugar.

In the early 1700s the demand for, and price of, sugar in Europe soared, as nearly all of the continent became addicted to sweets. In Saint-Domingue, sugar cultivation grew exponentially. In 1700 there were 18 sugar plantations on the island; at present (1791), there are nearly 300. The colony's population surpasses 500,000, including 465,000 slaves, 31,000 whites, and 28,000 free blacks and mulattoes. The most profitable plantations not only grow raw sugar, they also refine it: mashing the cane, boiling the juice repeatedly, and converting it into bricks of sugar for export. These are labor-intensive pursuits.

Despite a high mortality rate from disease, Saint-Domingue has become the most celebrated way for Frenchmen to make a fortune, either by running plantations or investing in them. For slaves, mortality rates are especially high; about half who arrive from Africa die within a few years. The key to a profitable plantation, many planters reason, is to work the slaves as hard as possible to ensure that their cost can be recouped before they die.

Because of the great discrepancy in population—in the parish of Acul, in the north, slaves outnumber whites 3,500 to 130—whites on the island have long feared a slave uprising. In 1758 an escaped slave named Mackandal, accused of leading a slave rebellion, was burned on a plank in the public square of Le Cap, the principal city of Saint-Domingue. As the flames scorched the ropes and the logs around him collapsed, he was momentarily set free, causing the blacks in the crowd to shout that he had been saved. Pandemonium ensued. Though soldiers cleared the square and threw Mackandal back into the fire, rumors long circulated that he had escaped to the mountains and was plotting a new rebellion.

From the 1770s onward, race relations on the island have been complicated by the rising status and wealth of many free blacks. The earliest French settlers, most of them men, had sexual relationships with black women. Not infrequently, these unions became permanent, produced children, and, as provided by French law, the women and children were freed. When the men died, their wives and children often inherited the land and property. Free blacks served in the French army that defended the colony, and they even participated in French military expeditions elsewhere, including supporting the American revolutionaries in the 1770s. The free blacks also served in the *maréchaussée*, charged with the task of rounding up runaway slaves and preserving order on the island. Three years ago, in 1788, French abolitionists established the Friends of the Blacks society in Paris. A few months later, another club, composed mostly of absentee planters, founded the Club Massiac to oppose the Friends of the Blacks. When word of these developments reached Saint-Domingue, chaos ensued. Some free blacks demanded political rights; slaves, who somehow caught wind of the changes in France, contemplated rebellion; some whites supported the French radicals, while many more sought to preserve slavery.

In July 1789, when the Third Estate became the National Assembly, it admitted six deputies from Saint-Domingue. When word of the storming of the Bastille reached Saint-Domingue, the poor whites on the island, wearing the red bonnet of the revolutionaries, marched in support of the Jacobins. Promulgation of the *Declaration of the Rights of Man* caused a sensation on the island in its echoes of Rousseau: "Men are born and remain equal in rights." Although other provisions of the *Declaration* accept "social distinctions" and define property as a "sacred and inviolable right," slaveholders knew that the document would destabilize the island. Within weeks, large bands of slaves had emerged to threaten several plantations.

As the king's officials abandoned the island, evidence of the general evaporation of the previous system of order, colonial assemblies emerged and almost instantly limited the vote to whites. The free blacks protested their exclusion and gained increasing support in the French National Assembly from Abbé Grégoire, a prominent Jacobin leader and member of the Friends of the Blacks, and from Alexandre Lameth, a prominent Feuillant. The Colonial Ministry and the white-dominated colonial assemblies vigorously protested; eventually the National Assembly decided to let the white-dominated assembly of Saint-Domingue sort the matter out.

By late 1790 the situation in Saint-Domingue became even more volatile. A mulatto leader, Ogé, supported by British abolitionists, fomented a slave uprising in the mountains of Saint-Domingue, which was put down. In October, Ogé was tortured to death in Le Cap. In Paris, word of his execution strengthened the Friends of the Blacks; on May 15, 1791, the French National Assembly granted political rights to mulattoes born of two free parents. The six delegates to the National Assembly from Saint-Domingue stormed out in protest. Just a few days ago, when word of the "May 15 Decree," as it became known, reached Saint-Domingue, the island was in an uproar.

Will the poor whites rise against the wealthy white planters and newly resurgent mulattoes? Will the slaves rise up against the planters? Will Saint-Domingue slip into chaos? And if so, what will happen to France? Saint-Domingue is the most valuable colony in the world; the French ports of Bordeaux, Brest, and Marseilles are heavily dependent on the sugar and coffee trade from the island; indeed, much of France's maritime economy would be severely damaged, perhaps even collapse, without the wealth generated by Saint-Domingue. Colonial and metropolitan France may be inseparable.

PART 3: THE GAME

MAJOR ISSUES FOR DEBATE

Members of the National Assembly, supported (or harassed) by the leaders of the sections in the back of the room, will be remaking France by drafting a new constitution. Will power, as in the past, be embodied in multiple separate institutions—the Catholic Church, the king and the nobility, the guilds and local parlements? Or will the French do as Rousseau proposes and establish a new type of society, embodied in the sovereign power of the General Will of the people themselves? While the National Assembly debates the fundamental constitution of the French nation, the members must also address innumerable issues of day-to-day governance, such as strengthening the economy and raising revenue for the government; securing order within Paris and building an army and navy capable of resisting foreign invasion; and determining the role of women in a revolutionary society and the status of slaves in the colonies. Delegates from factions will be reaching out to persuade undecided (or indeterminate) members of the Assembly, and also to strengthen their own positions by forming strategic alliances with other factions.

Pertaining to the Church

Civil Constitution of the Clergy. The National Assembly has already passed the CCC (July 1790), which the king signed last December. But it has yet to be formally added to the final Constitution of 1791. The main issue: should the Catholic Church be placed under the administrative and financial supervision of the National Assembly, or should it be controlled by the pope in Rome and his administrators (archbishops, bishops, and priests)?

Obligatory Oath. Although the Civil Constitution of the Clergy is now law, nearly half of France's Catholic priests have yet to swear the required oath obliging them to be "faithful to the nation, to the law, and to the king, and to maintain with all their power the constitution decreed by the National Assembly and accepted by the king." Should priests who refuse to take the oath be punished and, if so, how?

The Decree on Church Lands. The confiscation and sale of church lands was passed and implemented even before the Civil Constitution of the Clergy. The sale of church lands has been the main source of revenue for the revolutionary government. But the pope and religious conservatives regard this confiscation as theft of their property. Should the Decree on Church Lands be revoked or modified?

Pertaining to the King and the National Assembly

The Royal Sanction. This, too, was approved before; but should the "Royal Sanction" (or the king's Suspensive Veto), which allows the king to veto any legislation for a period of up to five years, be included in the final draft of the Constitution of 1791?

Unicameral Legislature. Many regard the National Assembly as an embodiment of the will of the French people, which should never be divided. But some political theorists, including Montesquieu (and Edmund Burke), believe in systems of checks and balances. The Constitution of the United States, for example, divides its legislature into two units: a House of Representatives and a Senate. Should the Constitution of France, as at present, remain unicameral, consisting of a single legislative body (the National Assembly), or should it have multiple houses?

The Abolition of Feudalism. Should all vestiges of noble rank and privilege be eliminated? This question, like many others, concerns the method and pace of change. Is it best to eliminate the vestiges of the past and rebuild society from the ground up, as Rousseau suggests? Or does society progress best through small, incremental changes, in order to ensure that the past is adapted to the present and future, as Edmund Burke proposes?

Pertaining to the Rights of Man

A Right to Property. Should the *Declaration of the Rights of Man* affirm that property is "a sacred and inviolable right" (Article 17)?

The Rights of Women. Does Article 1 of the *Declaration of the Rights of Man*—"Men are born and remain free and equal in rights"—apply to women?

Violence and Social Progress. Should Article 2 of the *Declaration of the Rights of Man*—which includes "resistance to oppression" as among the "natural rights of man"—be retained? Is violence ever justified in the pursuit of political ends? How does one determine legitimacy in terms of the use of force?

Pertaining to Governance

Distinguishing between Active and Passive Citizens. Will the National Assembly retain the law that gives more political rights, including that of serving in the National Guard, to "active citizens," which means those who own enough property to pay a small tax? If so, will "passive citizens," who pay no taxes, be denied all of these rights, or just some of them?

> **TIP**
>
> All of the members of the National Assembly are already in the group of active citizens.

Should the National Assembly revoke the law that distinguishes between "active" and "passive" citizens?

Slavery in Saint-Domingue. When word of the *Declaration of the Rights of Man* ("men are born free and equal in rights") spread to the slave colony in the Caribbean, it precipitated unrest. The free blacks (called "mulattoes") of the island demanded political rights, and slaves increasingly rebelled against their white masters. But at a time of economic chaos within France, the lucrative sugar and coffee plantations of Saint-Domingue remain central to the French economy. As Antoine Pierre Barnave, a Feuillant leader (and possibly a character in this game), explained in March 1790, "the interest of the French nation" lies in "supporting its commerce" and favoring the prosperity of its colonies. Regardless, should the National Assembly outlaw slavery in Saint-Domingue?

Threat of the Émigrés and Foreign Monarchs. The king's younger brothers, the Comte de Provence and the Comte d'Artois, have fled France and installed themselves as leaders of a government in exile in Coblenz, a city in a German state near the French border. They are organizing an army of émigré noblemen with the intent of invading France, restoring order in Paris, and deposing the National Assembly. Other European monarchs—including the Emperor of Austria (Leopold II, the brother of Marie Antoinette)—are known to oppose the French Revolution. Should France declare war on the émigré noblemen and on the foreign monarchies? Or should it avoid war at all costs? What should France's military preparation entail?

OBJECTIVES AND VICTORY CONDITIONS

Most players "win" by achieving the victory goals outlined in their factional advisory sheets. Some players' goals are unique to their characters, and some players—as in life—have secret victory objectives. Most players achieve their victory goals by persuading the National Assembly to establish a constitution and other laws that will help realize their vision for France. Some players may focus on the mechanics of building coalitions to pass specific measures; but the wisest course is to persuade the Indeterminates—those players who are not committed to any faction at the outset—that your overall philosophy best reflects what is best for France. Jacobins and the section leaders of Paris will emphasize various aspects of the philosophy of Jean-Jacques Rousseau; conservatives will likely endorse the views of Edmund Burke, as found in his *Reflections on the Revolution in France*. Several other key texts, including edited portions of the current constitution and the *Declaration of the Rights of Man*, appear in the appendices to this volume. A key to winning the game is to understand these major texts—their weaknesses as well as strengths.

Victory also requires that players understand the complicated—and fluid—situation within France. Players must master a range of historical contexts, ranging from the traditional role of the Catholic Church in France to the economics of slavery in Saint-Domingue, from the lack of tax revenue to the threat of foreign intervention. In giving speeches and writing papers, students must conduct additional research to support their arguments.

Indeterminates are obliged to listen carefully to all arguments, ask questions, and seek clarifications. While some may also pursue particular goals, they are largely free to vote on most issues in a manner that seems most consistent with the context of their historical role. But by the final session of the game, they must take positions on every issue and explain their reasons for doing so. These players should plan on a speech in the final Game Session, in which they explain why they have come to support one side or another.

Victory Determined at End of Game

"Victory" is determined when the final Game Session has concluded—but not before. If, for example, the Jacobins succeed in passing the Civil Constitution of the Clergy in the first session, but it is rescinded in the last Game Session, then the Jacobins have failed to achieve that particular goal.

In the event that the National Assembly completes and approves, by majority vote, a constitution, and if it is signed by the king, then it becomes law immediately. But the game does not end until the final Game Session has concluded.

RULES AND PROCEDURES

The National Assembly

Seating. The king's riding academy has been converted to the meeting place of the National Assembly, referred to as the *Manège*. This means that a podium has been erected at the front of the room, and galleries for the public are in the back and along the sides. The delegates of the National Assembly sit in the main area facing the podium. From the perspective of a speaker at the podium, the Jacobin faction must sit on the left, the Feuillants in the center, and the conservatives on the right. At the outset of the game, Indeterminates should sit toward the center of the National Assembly. But after the first session or two, they may sit wherever they wish—right, left, or center—and they may change their seats at will. Lafayette may sit wherever he wishes. The king should not sit near the galleries—or among the delegates of the National Assembly. The king may wish to negotiate with the President of the Assembly for suitable seating. If this cannot be worked out to the satisfaction of each player, the Gamemaster (instructor) will determine where the king should sit. The section leaders of the *sans-culottes* of Paris will sit in the galleries (chairs around the edge of the room, or perhaps in the last row).

Choosing a President. During the last few minutes of the final "setup" session, the Gamemaster will arrange the room as outlined above and ask everyone to take their seats. She will then ask for nominations for President of the National Assembly. Because the normal administrative machinery of the French government has largely evaporated, the National Assembly possesses considerable power; the President also wields some real executive power, chiefly through his ability to form committees and direct the course of legislation. Factions may nominate someone for President of the National Assembly. The Gamemaster will list the names and call for a vote. If no candidate receives a majority of votes, the candidate with the smallest number of votes will be eliminated and a run-off vote will be held, until one delegate receives an absolute majority. That delegate will become the Assembly's President.

TIP

The Gamemaster will provide the President with a special packet containing additional rules and guidance.

Removing the President. In eighteenth-century France, the presidency of the National Assembly changed hands fairly often; frequent elections would disrupt the game, however, and waste time. Therefore, the first President of the National Assembly will hold the position for the duration of the game, except in either of the following circumstances:

- The President may be removed at any time by a majority vote of the National Assembly; to avoid wasting time, a motion to request a vote to remove the President must first come in the form of a written note to the Gamemaster bearing the signatures of members representing at least 200 delegates (more, in a large class). The Gamemaster will then call the roll. If a challenger receives more votes than any other candidate, he will assume the presidential duties immediately.

- The President will be removed if he loses all of his delegates (see "Voting and Delegate Totals," below); a new election is then held immediately.

Voting and Delegate Totals. When the President considers discussion complete on a particular measure, he will announce a vote, asking delegates to stand to signify "yes" or "no." Delegates will likely vote by holding aloft their placards, which indicate how many votes they control. (At the outset of the

TIP

Any member of the National Assembly or the king may propose legislation, make comments, or give speeches, but only delegates are legally entitled to vote.

TIP

A delegate who has no remaining "votes" ceases to be a delegate; the GM will likely assign him a new role.

TIP

If the President persists in neglecting those at the podium, the GM will issue a warning that the President must "respect the podium." If, following the warning, the President continues to neglect those at the podium, the GM may impose penalties on the President.

game, each delegate is presumed to be an effective leader and speaker with forty-nine followers who vote along with him, following his lead. So each delegate, in voting, initially casts fifty votes, although there are a couple of exceptions.) Players may acquire more "followers"—and votes—by writing good articles and delivering effective speeches; conversely, they may lose supporters—and votes—by failing to speak well or write effective essays. Anyone who simply reads a speech aloud will automatically turn off supporters. Sometimes delegates may gain or lose support for other reasons as well.

Procedures. The President of the National Assembly will conduct the sessions as he sees fit and respect podium rule, but he must pointedly reject English contrivances such as Roberts' Rules of Order. This means that if any member of the National Assembly or the king lines up to speak at the podium, the President must allow him or her to speak. The GM will, if necessary, remind the President that someone is at the podium.

Functions of the National Assembly. The National Assembly has very broad legislative powers. There are two main types of issues that confront the National Assembly as it legislates:

- **Ratifying a Constitution.** By the summer of 1791, all of the various elements of the constitution are being assembled into a single, final document. This means that issues that arose earlier in the process can and will be reconsidered. Many provisions that have already been "adopted" (such as the Civil Constitution of the Clergy, the "Royal Sanction," and the *Declaration of the Rights of Man*) are being debated for a final time; these may now be rejected or modified by the National Assembly.

- **Governing the Nation.** Even as it finalizes the constitution, the National Assembly must also attend to the daily problems of governing and maintaining order in the nation. The Assembly may pass whatever legislation it chooses; for example, it may declare war on the United States, choose the squirrel as the national animal, try a delegate (or the king!) in court, or set wages and prices in Paris.

Many Frenchmen and -women regard a majority vote of the National Assembly as legally binding—and as an embodiment of the General Will, as prescribed by Rousseau. This gives the pronouncements of the Assembly considerable moral force. But mere passage of a law does not guarantee that the law will have force outside of the *Manège*. If, for example, the National Assembly orders all priests to take the Obligatory Oath, some priests may refuse to do so.

The National Assembly also chooses the commander of the National Guard. (At the outset of the game, Lafayette, a prominent delegate of the National Assembly, is also commander of the National Guard.) The National Assembly can replace the commander of the National Guard using the same procedure as is used to replace the President, described above.

According to the provisions of the current constitution, executive authority rests with the king and his ministers. But very little tax revenue is now flowing into the Finance Ministry. Most of the revenue for running the government is coming from the sale of Church lands. It is often uncertain whether the ministers who head up the government agencies will heed the directives of the king, who is nominally their boss, or of the National Assembly, which has access to funding. The king may, for example, declare war—a power given to him by the current draft of the constitution—but the National Assembly may vote against the declaration. The king's ministers of the Army, Navy, and War Ministry would likely be unsure of which instructions to follow, especially if the vote in the National Assembly was a close one. This may cause the old ministries to cease functioning.

The Crowd

The Crowd watches the debates from the galleries. They may add commentary or signal their approval or disapproval of the proceedings by, for example, cheering, jeering, clapping, or stomping their feet. They may not speak from the podium without express permission, however, as the podium rules only apply to legislative delegates and not to the section leaders or the Crowd. The President of the National Assembly may grant section leaders the right to speak if they ask, especially if he is aware of their power and influence. If the Crowd does not observe orderly rules of conduct, the Gamemaster may function, at the direction of the President, as a military officer within the National Assembly to guarantee the integrity of the proceedings. If the National Assembly does not appear to be a place where the Crowd can make its desires known, members of the Crowd may wish to move their action to the streets, where they can call the people to assemble and be heard by a more sympathetic audience. This may involve asking the Gamemaster to move the sphere of action to the streets temporarily so that a speech to the people can be heard in the class, or it might involve using the power of mass uprisings.

The Many Functions of the Gamemaster

Sometimes, the GM functions as a cheerleader, encouraging factions and individuals to work hard to win the game. Sometimes she functions as an instructor, explaining to students how they can give more effective speeches and research and write better papers. She may also perform other functions, including (but not limited to) the following:

Playing the Roles of Figures Outside of France. Although this game is set in the National Assembly in Paris, people outside of France may figure prominently in the game. These include:

- Pope Pius VI, at the Vatican

- Emperor Leopold II of Austria (the brother of Marie Antoinette, Queen of France); Frederick William II, Emperor of Prussia; Catherine of Russia; and Gustavus III of Sweden

- Marie Antoinette, the wife of Louis XVI. Note: it may seem that the wife of the king and mother of his children would share his goals, but that is not necessarily the case. Thus players may correspond with the queen—that is, the Gamemaster—and "she" may choose not to disclose that correspondence to the king.

- The Comte de Provence and the Comte d'Artois, the king's brothers (in Coblenz, a German principality); George Washington, president of the United States, or secretary of state Thomas Jefferson, at the nation's capital in Philadelphia, Pennsylvania.

- Edmund Burke, member of the English Parliament (House of Commons) for the Whig Party and author of *Reflections on the Revolution in France* (1790)

- The Duke of Orléans, also known as the Duke Egalité

Players who wish the assistance of such historical figures may do so by writing a letter to them and delivering it to the Gamemaster. Some examples:

"Dear President Washington, I trust all is well with you and Martha. I remember well our delightful evenings when we warmed ourselves by campfires, while fighting to liberate the American people from the tyranny of British rule. As you know, that war thrust the French government deeply into debt. I now ask the American people to reciprocate the generosity of the French over a decade ago by loaning the French government some 20 million dollars. . . . Yours in defense of democracy, Lafayette"

"Dear Pope Pius VI, I know that you opposed the Civil Constitution of the Clergy, and that you opposed as well my reluctant decision to sign that law. I had little choice but to bend to the will—"General Will" as they term it these days— of the French people. I ask that you, too, reduce opposition to the Catholic Church by allowing the Catholic clergy to take the oath of allegiance to me—their king—and to the National Assembly. Yours in Christ, Louis XVI, Rex"

The Gamemaster will likely respond to such letters, though this may take some time.

Initiatives within France. The Gamemaster will also adjudicate various issues that may arise outside the National Assembly, whether that be in Paris, the countryside of France, or the nations of Europe. If, for example, non-juring Catholic priests foment a rebellion in Provence and if the National Assembly orders the National Guard to put it down, then the GM determines the chances that the National Guard will succeed, rolls a die, and announces the outcome.

The Gamemaster News Service. The Gamemaster will provide some clues as to "where" the class is in real history by issuing Gamemaster News Service updates periodically. For example, the Gamemaster News Service might indicate that a ship has sailed into Rouen with word that Virginia ratified the Bill of Rights on December 15, 1791 and became the eleventh state to do so. This means that more than two-thirds of American states have ratified the Bill of Rights, making it part of the Constitution of the United States. It also indicates that your game has likely moved into early 1792. Remember, however, that time within France *after* July 1791 does not necessarily unfold according to history, because players may change that history. But history in Virginia, or elsewhere in the world, is less likely to be changed by your class's activities in France after July 1, 1791.

TIP

Players improve their chances of persuading the Gamemaster (for example: as Washington or as Pius VI) to do what they wish if they submit evidence that those historical figures did in fact behave, or would be inclined to behave, in the way that players propose.

BASIC OUTLINE OF THE GAME

The game has several phases: Setup, Game Play, and Postmortem.

Preparatory Sessions

SESSION 1

IDEAS IN FERMENT: FROM THE ENLIGHTENMENT TO ROUSSEAU

Required Reading:

- Read Prologue; skim the background and basic rules.

- Historical Background: Versailles to Varennes: The French Revolution from the Ancien Régime to July 1, 1791, pp. 19–43.

- Montesquieu, excerpts from *The Spirit of the Laws* (1748), pp. 88–93.

- Voltaire, excerpts from "Law, Religion and the State" and "Liberty and Fundamental Laws" (1764), pp. 94–98.

- Rousseau, excerpts from *Emile* (1762), pp. 98–99.

- Rousseau, excerpts from *First Discourse* (1750), pp. 99–107.

Class Activities: Discussion

- The Historical Background section of this game book emphasizes a number of causes of the French Revolution. What are some of them? How do they work together to create a widespread sense that the French government needs massive change?

- French citizens' demands for change are founded on Enlightenment criticisms of absolutism, but they are given a forum because of economic problems that precipitated the calling of the Estates General. Many of these problems, including the near bankruptcy of the French state, cannot be addressed merely by the creation of a more representative government. What problems will confront any type of government in 1789? Which ones are specific to the Ancien Régime?

- There are many different ideas among the citizenry about the best course of action for the French government. What are some of these conflicting visions? On what points do they agree or disagree?

- Church and King both become symbols of privilege and oppression. Why? Can you imagine a way in which each institution could join the revolutionary movement? What changes would be required to their beliefs or mode of existence?

- At what historical moments do ordinary people, rather than deputies, change the path of the Revolution? What are the people's concerns and how do they make themselves known?

- Montesquieu believes that good governments entail a separation of powers. How does this idea constitute a criticism of the absolute rule of the French monarchy?

- Rousseau argues in his *First Discourse* that Enlightenment thought has enshrined reason and destroyed human decency; people treated each other better when they weren't burdened with academic knowledge and religious skepticism. In a state of nature, people lived simpler and kinder lives, infused with purposeful spirituality. In *Emile*, Rousseau tries to devise a system of education that will help educate young people without indoctrinating them into the soulless and sterile world of society and academia. Is the Enlightenment—best exemplified by the rise of medicine and the sciences—superior to Rousseau's spiritual purity in a state of nature?

SESSION 2

THE REVOLUTION BEGINS: UP TO JULY 1, 1791

Required Reading

- Historical Background: Versailles to Varennes: The French Revolution from the Ancien Régime to July 1, 1791, pp. 19–43.

- Sieyès, "What is the Third Estate?" (1789), pp. 108–111.

- "Declaration of the King upon the Estates General" (1789), pp. 115–117.

- "August Decrees" (1789), pp. 117–120.

Class Activities: Discussion and Distribution of Two Roles

- Why was Louis XVI obliged to convene the Estates General and why did the Third Estate—the commoners—insist that they alone were the legislative body of France?

- Why does Louis XVI oppose the Third Estate's goal of establishing itself as the National Assembly of France? Why does he eventually agree to this?

- What revolutionary developments unfold from July 1, 1789, through June 30, 1791?

- GM distributes the roles of Louis XVI and Lafayette.

ROUSSEAU'S GENERAL WILL, THE *DECLARATION OF THE RIGHTS OF MAN*, AND BURKE'S SEARING CRITIQUE

Required Reading

- Rousseau's *Social Contract* (1762), a separate text assigned by your instructor.

- Burke's excerpts from *Reflections on the Revolution in France*, pp. 145–167.

- *Declaration of the Rights of Man and of the Citizen* (August 26, 1789), pp. 120–123.

Class Activities: Discussion and Distribution of Roles

- How does Rousseau's "General Will" allow people both the benefits of living in society and complete freedom from external compulsion?

- Edmund Burke denounces Rousseau's notion of creating an entirely new society based on the General Will. What arguments does he marshal in opposition to Rousseau? And to the French revolutionaries?

- How does the *Declaration of the Rights of Man and of the Citizen* reflect the ideas of Rousseau? How does it differ?

- GM distributes all of the remaining roles.

PREPARING FOR THE NATIONAL ASSEMBLY SESSION

Required Reading

- Your role sheet (both your private, personal biography and, if you belong to a faction, your faction's statement).

- Biographies of all of the figures in the game. It is advisable to educate yourself about your friends and allies, your foes, and those who may be persuaded to support "your" views.

- The "Origin of the Jacobin Club," pp. 123–125.

- The game rules.

Class Activities: Faction Meetings or a Quiz on the Readings

During the final ten minutes, the Assembly meets briefly to elect the President of the National Assembly.

- GM presides, and distributes additional role sheets to the President.

- GM also distributes the Gamemaster News Service One.

the Game Sessions, the Assembly will debate a set of issues determined in advance by the President of the National Assembly. See "Procedures of the National Assembly" (p. 52) for the general rules during these sessions.

GAME SESSION 1

THE ROLE OF THE CATHOLIC CHURCH

The class may also consider other issues, as determined by the President.

Required Reading

- Whatever sources—from the game book as well as independent research—you need to support your spoken and written arguments.

- "August Decrees," pp. 117–120.

- The Decrees on Church Lands and Monastic Vows (November to February, 1789), pp. 125–126.

- The Civil Constitution of the Clergy (July 12, 1790), pp. 128–132.

- The Obligatory Oath (November 27, 1790), p. 133.

- *Charitas: [Papal Statement] On the Civil Oath in France* (April 13, 1791), pp. 133–136.

Class Activities

- Distribution of newspapers, first issue.

- Meeting of the National Assembly, with likely debates on the role of the Catholic Church in France. Note: although the National Assembly has already passed the Civil Constitution and other measures, these measures have not been formally added to the Constitution of 1791. This session has been convened to decide, among other issues as determined by the President, whether the Civil Constitution will be included with the Constitution or if the Civil Constitution (and its related decrees) will be modified.

- End of session: the President requests agenda suggestions and announces the agenda for the next National Assembly meeting.

Note that players who do not belong to one of the four factions will have separate writing dead-lines and requirements; these should be discussed with the instructor/GM.

GAME SESSION 2

TOPIC PRE-DETERMINED BY PRESIDENT

Required Reading

- Decree Abolishing the Nobility (June 19, 1790), p. 128.
- Constitution of 1791, pp. 136–145.

Class Activities

- National Assembly: debates are moderated by the President.
- End of session: the President requests agenda suggestions and announces the agenda for the next National Assembly meeting.
- Gamemaster distributes Gamemaster News Service Two.

GAME SESSION 3

Suggested Reading

Reread pertinent sections of the game book; also conduct independent research to strengthen your essay and arguments.

Class Activities

- Distribution of newspapers, second issue.
- National Assembly: debate on various matters. If the President did not announce topics at the end of the previous session, assume that they will include the Royal Sanction and matters pertaining to the nobility.
- End of session: the President requests agenda suggestions and announces the agenda for the next National Assembly meeting.

GAME SESSION 4

Suggested Reading

- Decree Regarding Membership in the National Guard (June 12, 1790), pp. 126–127.

- Reread *Declaration of the Rights of Man*, pp. 120–123.

Class Activities

- National Assembly: debate on various matters. If the President did not announce topics at the end of the previous session, assume that they will include the *Declaration of the Rights of Man*, active and passive citizenship, and admission to the National Guard.

- End of session: the President requests agenda suggestions and announces the agenda for the next National Assembly meeting.

- GM distributes Gamemaster News Service Three.

GAME SESSION 5

Suggested Reading

- Jacobins and the section leaders (the Crowd) should reread Burke's *Reflections on the Revolution in France* to better understand (and refute) the conservative arguments; conservatives should reread Rousseau's *Social Contract* to better understand (and refute) the radical arguments.

Class Activities

- Distribution of newspapers, third issue.

- National Assembly: debate on various matters. If the President did not announce topics at the end of the previous session, assume that they will include the slave rebellion in Saint-Domingue and the situation in Europe.

- End of session: the President requests agenda suggestions and announces the agenda for the next National Assembly meeting.

Suggested Reading

Read whatever supports your position and will help you win the game.

Class Activities

- National Assembly: debate on various matters. Game ends.

- GM distributes handout: "What Really Happened after July 1, 1791."

Note: Some classes may include additional Game Sessions, and some may include fewer. Your instructor will explain any changes to the deadlines for written assignments.

POSTMORTEM SESSION(S)

DEBRIEFING THE GAME

Required Reading

- Handout from the end of the previous class: "What Really Happened after July 1, 1791."

Class Activities

- The Gamemaster will revert to the role of instructor; players will formally renounce their game names and become their "real" selves again.

- The instructor will encourage a general discussion of what transpired during the game. Students may wish to explain their goals and strategies. Indeterminates should explain why they chose to support one or another faction.

- The class will discuss what really happened in France after July 1, 1791—and why "their" history diverged from the real history, if it did.

- Students should share their personal beliefs about whether Rousseau or Burke was more nearly "right."

- Some classes may watch (and discuss) *Danton,* a movie focusing on the later stages of the game, and beyond.

ASSIGNMENTS AND GRADING

ADVISORY

Students are expected to support their written and spoken views with more facts and other forms of evidence than are contained in this game book. This means that for most papers, students must conduct research to strengthen their work. The game book contains a select bibliography; many other issues can be researched online. The French Revolution is one of the great subjects of historical inquiry.

This game requires that students advance their objectives by writing papers, giving speeches, and conducting negotiations. For players in the four main factions, the main writing assignments will consist of articles that will appear in the faction's newspaper, which will be published several times during the game (the actual number of issues will depend on the length of the game). The writing assignments (and victory objectives) of the Indeterminates or other players will be specified in their role sheets. The instructor will announce the total number of pages that each student must write for the game, and also indicate the relative importance of each type of assignment (for example, written work may comprise two-thirds of the grade and class participation one-third).

Players are expected to speak frequently during the game. Sometimes they will speak extemporaneously in response to debates or negotiations, and at other times they will give speeches from the podium. Reading speeches aloud is discouraged; those who do so will likely receive grade penalties and reductions in their delegate totals.

PART 4: **ROLES AND FACTIONS**

ROLE ASSIGNMENTS

Players are assigned roles based on actual historical figures. All of the possible historical figures in the game are indicated in the section that follows. Unless your class is very large, it will probably have fewer players—and fewer historical figures represented. Not all classes will include the same configuration of historical figures. This helps explain why your game may differ greatly from a French Revolution game played by another class. Your Gamemaster will tell you which figures appear in the game (and you may wish to cross out those who do not appear).

The historical figures can be divided into three types:

1. Major essential figures (Louis XVI and Lafayette)

2. Members of four major factions

3. Indeterminates.

LIST OF ALL POSSIBLE PLAYERS

Unless otherwise noted, all players are members of the National Assembly

Major Roles; no Explicit Faction

- Louis XVI, King of France (presides over the National Assembly)
- Marquis de Lafayette, Commander of the National Guard

Conservative Faction

- Jean-Sifrein Maury (non-juring clergy)
- Jacques Antoine Marie de Cazalès (nobility)
- Antoine-Éléonor-Léon Leclerc de Juigné, Archbishop of Paris (non-juring clergy)
- Count of Clermont (nobility)
- Denis Bérardier (non-juring clergy)
- Trophime-Gérard Lally (nobility)
- Duke of Liancourt (nobility)

Feuillant Faction

- Emmanuel Joseph Sieyès (juring clergy)
- Jean-Sylvain Bailly, Mayor of Paris
- Bertrand Barère (editor, *The Point of the Day*)
- Antoine Pierre Joseph Marie Barnave
- Alexandre-Théodore-Victor Lameth
- Jean-François Ducos
- Jean Joseph Mounier

Jacobin Faction

- Henri-Baptiste Grégoire (juring clergy)
- Marie-Jean Hérault de Séchelles
- Jérôme Pétion de Villeneuve
- François Nicolas Léonard Buzot
- Jean Bon Saint-André
- Louis Antoine Léonde Saint-Just (not a member of the National Assembly)
- Camille Desmoulins (editor, *Revolutions of France and Brabant*)
- Maximilien Robespierre
- Jacques-Louis David (painter)

Section Leaders of Paris/the Crowd (none are members of the National Assembly)

- Georges Jacques Danton, Cordeliers leader
- Anne-Marguerite Andalle (female)
- Jean-Paul Hébert (editor, *Father Duchesne* [*Père Duchesne*])
- Pauline Léon (female)
- Jean-Paul Marat (editor, *The Friend of the People*)
- Françoise Rolin (female)
- Jean-Françoise Varlet
- Françoise-Noel Babeuf

Indeterminates

- François Louis Hutteau (journalist)
- François Anne Jacques Bouron
- Thomas Verny
- Jean-Baptiste Alquier
- Etta Palm d'Aelders (female; not a member of the National Assembly)
- Claude Périer
- Charles Polverel (surgeon)
- Jean Blampain
- Etienne Lucy
- Jean Guineau Dupré

A List of All Figures with Brief Biographies

Most of the biographical accounts (except those for Louis XVI and Lafayette) are brief; you may wish to do further research. But remember: nothing that you read in history books that happened to these figures after July 1, 1791, will necessarily occur in the game. After July 1, all of the historical figures in the game may behave in different ways than they did in history.

The Two Major Figures: Louis XVI and Lafayette

Louis XVI. Louis XVI, 36, is the king of France, the fifth monarch in the Bourbon line. In 1770, when he was sixteen, his grandfather promoted France's alliance with Austria by arranging for Louis's marriage to Marie Antoinette, daughter of Maria-Theresa, archduchess of Austria. Marie Antoinette was fourteen. In 1774, Louis's grandfather died and Louis became king; he was twenty-one. He was crowned in the cathedral at Rheims.

Keenly interested in foreign affairs, Louis played a major role in the French decision to intervene on behalf of the American colonies in their "revolutionary war" against Great Britain. The cost of the war exacerbated France's perennial budget problems. On the advice of the Swiss banker and financier Jacques Necker, Louis in 1788 decided to convene the Estates General, which, per French legal precedent, was necessary before the crown could impose new taxes.

In June 1789, to Louis's chagrin, the "Third Estate" declared itself to be the legislative body of France—the National Assembly. His attempts to cow it into submission, however, failed when the people of Paris, in a massive upheaval, stormed the Bastille. The emergence of the National Guard of Paris, under the command of Lafayette and the National Assembly, provided an effective counterweight to the king's soldiers and ensured the survival of the National Assembly. In October 1789, after the market women had besieged the king at Versailles and forced him to the Tuileries Palace in Paris, he and his family became virtual prisoners.

Under pressure from the National Assembly, Louis took an oath to support the constitution enacted by the National Assembly. In December 1790 he signed the Civil Constitution of the Clergy, which made all Catholic officials employees of the state and ultimately subject to the authority of the National Assembly. It also obliged Catholic officials to take an oath of loyalty to the constitution. Several months ago, Pope Pius VI repudiated the Civil Constitution of the Clergy and threatened to excommunicate those Catholics who adhered to its provisions. About half of the Catholic clergy in France have refused to take the oath and some who have taken it have since repudiated it. Rumors fly that the king takes mass privately with a non-juring priest.

Now, having been abducted from Paris, or perhaps having attempted to flee from it, the king and his family have been returned and placed "under protection" at the Tuileries.

Louis remains the titular head of the government. If the current draft of the constitution passes and he signs it into law, Louis will continue to exercise some executive functions, including the power to delay legislation by exercising a "suspensive veto." Overshadowing the political dispute over the future role of the king is the crowd of Paris which, on several occasions, has taken matters into its own hands and threatened, even nearly killed, the royal family.

Lafayette. Lafayette, 32, formerly the Marquis de La Fayette, is from one of the truly noble families of France. Lafayette's father, a captain, was shot and killed by the English at the Battle of Minden in 1759, when Lafayette was only 2 years old. His family owned huge estates that generated immense revenues, and the death of his mother and grandfather left the young Lafayette with an income of 120,000 *livres* (nearly a million dollars). At 17, he married Adrienne de Noailles, whose dowry was about 2 million dollars. Lafayette was one of the richest men in France.

Despite his wealth, however, Lafayette coveted a career in the military. When the Americans declared war on England in 1776, Lafayette volunteered to serve as a major general with General George Washington, commander of the American armies. After the British defeat at Saratoga, Lafayette's connections at Versailles helped persuade Louis XVI to enter the war on behalf of the Americans. Lafayette also served ably as a commander of the American forces that trapped Cornwallis at Yorktown.

During the years immediately following the American Revolution, Lafayette supported reform in France by joining a society that sought to eliminate slavery on the French colony of Saint-Domingue (Haiti). When Louis convoked the Estates General, Lafayette was elected as a member of the nobility (Second Estate). Though he took no public stand on whether all of the Estates should meet as a single body, he was elected vice president of the "National Assembly" after the king abandoned his opposition. The president immediately resigned and Lafayette took his place in the National Assembly, just when many feared the king would move against it militarily.

After the fall of the Bastille on July 14, 1789, Lafayette was named commanding general of the citizens' militia, which became known as the National Guard of Paris. Lafayette sought to regularize recruitment and ensure that the men would accept discipline. Eventually, the National Guard became a largely middle-class, volunteer organization.

Then came the Great Fear in the countryside, when peasants rose up against the nobility, attacking chateaux and burning the hated volumes that recorded ancient feudal dues. To preserve order in Paris, Lafayette took out a personal loan from his bankers to help pay the National Guard. The Paris Commune voted to give him a large salary, which he refused.

Lafayette found time to attend some sessions of the National Assembly. His draft of the *Declaration of the Rights of Man* bore many similarities to the final document passed by the National Assembly; and Lafayette came up with the current constitutional compromise (suspensive veto) whereby the king can veto any legislation of which he disapproves; if, however, two subsequent legislatures pass the legislation, it will become law.

During the riot of the market women on October 5, 1789, Lafayette nearly lost control of the National Guard. Lafayette arrived at Versailles just in time to prevent the wholesale butchery of the king and his family. The mob demanded that the king and his family return to Paris, and Lafayette tried to make the most of a difficult situation by forming a procession to escort the now-captive king to Paris.

In January 1790, Lafayette was offered command of all the National Guards, which he refused. During the winter of 1789–90, Lafayette declared, time and again, that the Revolution was over. In a speech in February, he called for an end to social upheaval throughout France: "For the Revolution, we needed disorders; the old order was nothing but slavery and, under those circumstances, insurrection is the holiest of duties, but for the Constitution, the new order must be stabilized, individuals must be secure. . . . The government must take on strength and energy." The speech alarmed royalists and radicals alike.

When the mob prevented the king and queen from celebrating mass at Saint-Cloud (April 1791), Lafayette barely managed to herd the royal family back into the Tuileries. Lafayette's impotence was further confirmed by the disappearance of the royal family on June 20, 1791. Lafayette had either been inattentive to his duties to protect the king from abductors or had collaborated in his escape. In any case, Lafayette ordered the National Guard to pursue the king. Radical leaders in the Assembly, especially the Jacobins, have been strident in their opposition to Lafayette. In recent weeks M. Danton at the Jacobin club intoned, "M. the commander-general promised on his head that the king would not leave; we must have the person of the king or the head of M. the commander-general." Some radicals now call not for a constitutional monarchy but for a republic.

Lafayette, though swamped by his duties as commander of the National Guard, continues to attend sessions of the National Assembly, though he no longer presides. He also controls many votes of loyal supporters in the Assembly.

Conservatives: Clergy and Nobility

Given the option of violating the instructions of the papal father or the laws of the National Assembly, many conservative clergy have chosen to adhere to their original vows of obedience to the Church and the pope. They have refused to take the oath in support of the Civil Constitution and the National Assembly. Although some Catholic Jansenists long to return to the primitive life of the early Christians, most conservative Catholics seek to overturn the Civil Constitution of the Clergy. They also regard the king as a traditional source of religious authority and stability.

Many of the nobles (originally of the Second Estate) who belong to the National Assembly had been sympathetic to joining the Third Estate. Most were among the exuberant deputies who in August 1789 renounced feudal privileges (Fourth of August Decrees) in the hopes of calming the upheaval in Paris and the countryside. But even as they made it clear that they were on the side of change, things slipped further toward chaos, and it seemed like change could not be fast or radical enough to please some people. In October, all Paris erupted and the market women went on a rampage to Versailles. Hundreds, perhaps thousands of aristocrats fled the country. Now members of the Jacobin Clubs throughout France hold festivals where they sing the blood-thirsty ditty, "Ça Ira" ("It'll happen"—see the Core Texts section, p. 123). The nobility regard the current constitution as an invitation to more bloodshed and violence. The National Assembly has all the real power; the king is a pitiable figurehead. The protection of property rights consists of mere words. Power is in the hands of an unstable legislature that happily condones violence.

Maury (more-REE). Jean-Sifrein Maury, 45, an official at a monastery in Lihons, was born near Avignon, the son of a cobbler. He studied theology and became a celebrated speaker and writer. In 1784 he was chosen as a member of the French Academy. In 1789 he was elected to the Estates General as a member of the First Estate (clergy). He has become a formidable defender of the Catholic Church and conservative principles in the National Assembly.

Cazalès (KAH-zah-lez). Jacques Antoine Marie de Cazalès, 34, a nobleman and cavalry officer from Toulouse, was elected to the Second Estate (nobility). In July 1789, he opposed the plan to combine the Three Estates into a single legislative body, which became the National Assembly. He has spoken repeatedly in defense of the monarchy. His vociferous criticism of deputy Barnave, who had sought to reduce the powers of the king, led to a duel in 1790. Barnave wounded Cazalès slightly.

Juigné (JWEE-knee), Archbishop of Paris. Antoine-Éléonor-Léon Leclerc de Juigné, 63, Archbishop of Paris, is the leading non-juring Catholic in France. The younger son of a noble family from Angers, in western France, de Juigné entered seminary in Paris and swiftly advanced in the Catholic Church. In 1781, at 53, he was appointed Archbishop of Paris. Elected to the First Estate, he promoted its amalgamation into the National Assembly in July 1789. He also renounced the church's rights to the feudal taxes and offered financial support to the National Assembly. But he has staunchly opposed most provisions of the Civil Constitution of the Clergy and has refused to take the "obligatory oath."

Clermont (CLAYR-mohn). Stanislas Marie Adélaïde, the Count of Clermont-Tonnerre, 34, army colonel, was born in Lorraine, near the Rhine. His family and that of his wife have large landholdings in northeastern France (Lorraine). Recently he founded the Monarchist Club in Paris and began printing a journal, the *Impartial Observer*. Barnave denounced both projects as part of a conspiracy and forced them to be shut down.

Bérardier (BAY-rard-dee-ay). Denis Bérardier, 56, scientist, philosopher, and theologian, received a doctorate in theology from the Sorbonne. He ran what had been a Jesuit school, where he attracted notice for his research on electricity. As a teacher at the College of Louis-le-Grand, he taught Camille Desmoulins, Maximilien Robespierre, and Luce de Lancival. With Robespierre's support, he became canon for Arras. In 1789 he was elected to the First Estate for Paris. He has recently published a book in defense of traditional Catholicism—and in opposition to the Civil Constitution of the Clergy—entitled *Principles of the Faith on the Government of the Church* (1791).

Lally (LAH-lee). Trophime-Gérard Lally-Tollendal, 40, is one of the most prominent members of the nobility. His father, the Count of Lally, the Viceroy of India, was blamed for the French defeat at Pondicherry and was executed. The son has labored to prove the unfairness of those charges. Elected by the nobility of Paris to the Estates General, the younger Lally was among the leaders of the group that joined with the Third Estate in June 1789. Though a monarchist, he has supported significant modifications in the Ancien Régime.

Liancourt (LEE-ahn-koor). François Alexandre Frédéric, Duke of Liancourt, 44, is of high noble birth with longstanding ties to the royal family. At twenty, though already a duke, he became an officer in the cavalry. In 1788, he was promoted to major general in the army. He has also been a proponent of educational reform and technical advancement, founding a school for poor children and building cotton mills in Liancourt. He does not seek to restore the Ancien Régime.

Feuillants

The Feuillants—as they call themselves—endorse the revolution and its accomplishments: the Civil Constitution of the Clergy; the abolition of feudalism; the replacement of monarchical power with a forceful unicameral legislature; the defense of property; and so on. Until just weeks ago, most Feuillants belonged to the Jacobins, but left the group out of fear that the elimination of the monarchy would result in societal collapse. Because the revolution is now complete, any further violence is wrong. The task, Feuillants say, is to reconcile the deeply divided people of France so that they can come together and build a strong nation. This, the Feuillants feel, requires a compromise: retention of the king, whose duties will be carefully circumscribed by a constitution. The Feuillants' goals are embedded in the current draft of the constitution. The Feuillants have an eye, too, to the future and to economic development of the nation. They believe that the "corporate" character of the Ancien Régime—the pervasive power of guilds, the influence of the Catholic Church, and the financial system of the French monarch—hindered the nation's economic growth. If France is to play a major role in the future, it must in some way approximate the more vigorous free-market institutions of England.

Sieyès (see-YEZ). Emmanuel Joseph Sieyès, 43, prominent Catholic official and essayist, was born in southern France, near Nice, studied at a seminary in Paris, and advanced rapidly in the Catholic Church. At 32, he became canon and vicar-general of the Cathedral at Chartres. His pamphlet, "What is the Third Estate?"—provided the fateful answer: "everything." This galvanized revolutionary sentiment. His sensational pamphlet provided the justification for the Third Estate's becoming the National Assembly in July 1789. Rejected to represent the First Estate, he was chosen by the Third Estate (commons) for Paris. In defiance of Pope Pius VI, he has taken the Obligatory Oath.

Bailly (BUY-yee). Jean-Sylvain Bailly, 55, the mayor of Paris, was born in Paris and, as a young man, became an astronomer. His essay on the satellites of Jupiter modified the conclusions of Galileo and Kepler. He was elected to the French Academy in 1783—and was chosen by the Third Estate to represent Paris. He was the first to sign the Tennis Court Oath. When the Third Estate called itself the National Assembly, he was chosen as its first president; on July 15, the day after the fall of the Bastille, he was elected mayor of Paris—a new position, and one he still holds.

Barère (BAR-err). Bertrand Barère, 35, lawyer and writer, was born in the foothills of the Pyrenees, near Spain, of well-to-do parents. He studied law at Toulouse and was admitted, at 23, to the Academy of the Floral Games, a well-regarded French literary society. He was elected to the Estates General as a deputy for the Third Estate and was among those who, in July 1789, advocated that it become the National Assembly, the sole legislative body of France. Although he supported the Jacobins in the early years, he recently left them to help form the Feuillant Club. He is editor of the journal *Le Point du Jour* [The Point of the Day], which reports on matters before the National Assembly.

Barnave (BAR-nawve). Antoine Pierre Joseph Marie Barnave, 29, lawyer and essayist, was born in Grenoble, the son of a lawyer. He served in the Parlement (king's court) in the region, encouraging it to take an independent stand from that of the king. He wrote essays attacking the king in 1788 and was elected to represent the commons in 1789. He supported the Third Estate's transformation into the National Assembly and defended the rioters who took control of Paris in July 1789. In recent months he was among the delegates who left the Jacobins to form the more moderate Feuillants.

Lameth (lah-MET). Alexandre-Théodore-Victor Lameth, 31, son of a noble family that owns large estates, became a soldier, served in the American Revolution, and retired (at 29!) in 1789. He helped found the Jacobin Club and also the Society of the Friends of Blacks, which promotes the rights of blacks in Saint-Domingue. Elected to the Third Estate, he endorsed its becoming the National Assembly. Alarmed by the increasing instability in Paris, he helped found the Feuillants. He seeks to unify the factions of France by means of a constitutional monarchy.

Ducos (DEW-koh). Jean-François Ducos, 25, grew up in Bordeaux and was sent to Nantes to prepare for a career in commerce. But he soon shifted his focus to literature and philosophy, especially the works of Rousseau, and gravitated to revolutionary ideas. Back in Bordeaux, he founded the Bordeaux Jacobin Club and its National Guard. Though many in Bordeaux, a port city dependent on the sugar trade, want to preserve slavery in Saint-Domingue, Ducos has joined the Society of the Friends of Blacks. Now, as unrest mounts, Ducos has come to Paris and become a leading figure at the Feuillant Club.

Mounier (moo-knee-AY). Jean Joseph Mounier, 32, was born in Grenoble, the son of a banker and cloth retailer. He became a lawyer and in 1783 acquired a judgeship, granting him noble status. After writing impassioned articles in support of the Third Estate, he was elected its representative. He became a leading figure, and sometimes the president, of the newly formed National Assembly. He has called for an end to the violence in Paris and moderated some of his earlier views.

Jacobins

The Jacobins, who took over the Jacobin monastery in Paris as their meeting place, consist mostly of lawyers, small-town notables and magistrates, and others who were familiar with the workings of the Ancien Régime and had thus come to despise it. The Jacobins approve of the achievements of the revolution at present, but they insist that more must be done. They applaud specifically the fact that the Catholic Church has been stripped of its feudal power and placed under the thumb of the National Assembly, and they have cheered the dismantling of noble powers and the tentative adoption of a unicameral (single) house legislature with significant powers. Unlike the United States and England, where the will of the people is divided into multiple houses (Senate and House of Representatives; Houses of Lords and Commons), the current constitution grants great power to a single legislature. The pending constitution also protects property rights, and this matters immensely to the many lawyers and shopkeepers who belong to the Jacobin Club. Now the Jacobins demand an end to the monarchy, which would plunge France into a radically different political world. The attempted flight of the king is proof, they say, of his perfidy, and all the more justification for an end to the monarchy and the beginning of a republic.

Grégoire (GRAY-gwah). Henri-Baptiste Grégoire, 41, juring Catholic priest and philosopher, was born in a hamlet in Lorraine, near the Rhine, the son of a tailor. He won a prize for an essay on poetry from the Academy of Nancy, entered a seminary at Metz, and was ordained at 24. Elected to the First Estate for Nancy, one of the few parish priests to be so honored, he took a major role in moving the First Estate to join with the Third Estate in June 1789. He was one of the first to take the Tennis Court Oath and to swear the Civil Oath, in accordance with the requirements of the Civil Constitution of the Clergy. He has also advocated abolishing slavery in Saint-Domingue.

Hérault (AIR-roh). Marie-Jean Hérault de Séchelles, 31, of an ancient noble family, studied law in Paris. In his twenties he became the King's Advocate and a favorite of the court, as well as Marie Antoinette. He also published books on oratory and on philosophy. He took part in the storming of the Bastille and became judge in a new court in Paris. He has spoken in support of a strong army of citizen-soldiers to defend the nation and the revolution.

Pétion (PAY-tee-on). Jérôme Pétion de Villeneuve, 35, the son of a wealthy lawyer from Chartres, studied law and became a minor government official in Orléans. But he soon distinguished himself as a writer, and his advanced views attracted a following in free-thinking circles. His "Essays on Marriage," which advocated the marriage of priests, caused a sensation and led to his election to the Third Estate for Chartres. He has become a staunch supporter of the Jacobins and an ally of Robespierre. He opposed the king's veto and was among the three delegates who were sent to bring the king and his family back from Varennes a few weeks ago.

Buzot (boo-ZOH). François Nicolas Léonard Buzot, 31, lawyer, the son of a prominent lawyer in Normandy and a noblewoman with family ties to the court, studied law in Paris and secured a position as a government lawyer in Normandy. He was elected to the Third Estate and, inspired by Rousseau, sought to realize that visionary's goal of a nation governed by the general will of a virtuous people. After 1789, he became a stalwart Jacobin.

Saint-André (sahn-TAHN-dray). Jean Bon Saint-André, 42, of an artisan family near Toulouse, studied navigation at Bordeaux and became a ship's captain and naval officer. In 1771 he studied theology in Switzerland and was ordained a Huguenot (Calvinist) minister, an office he practiced secretly. After ratification of the Edict of Toleration of 1788 allowed Protestant worship, Saint-André served openly as a Protestant minister. In 1790 he joined the Jacobin Club and strongly endorsed the Civil Constitution of the Clergy, partly because it would ensure protection of Protestants and others. Fearing attack from foreign monarchs as well, he seeks to strengthen the French army and especially its navy.

Saint-Just (SAHN-joos). Louis Antoine Léon de Saint-Just, just 24, the son of a soldier who was ennobled on account of his bravery, studied law at Reims and, eschewing a law degree, became a writer. His powerful denunciations of privilege, the monarchy, and the Catholic Church attracted the attention of radical theorists and politicians. In 1789 he joined the newly formed National Guard of Paris, commanded by Lafayette, and was promoted to Lieutenant Colonel in 1790. Though too young to vote in the National Assembly, he speaks there with passion and force. On every issue for which he gives a speech, 50 delegates will vote in support of his position.

Desmoulins (DAY-moo-lahn). Camille Desmoulins, 31, the son of a petty judge in northern France, received a scholarship to attend Louis-le-Grand, a prestigious school in Paris, where he met Maximilien Robespierre, a leading Jacobin deputy. He studied law in Paris, but, hindered by his stammer (which disappears when he speaks of human rights), shifted increasingly to journalism. His journal, *Les Revolutions de France et de Brabant* [*The Revolutions of France and the Austrian Netherlands*], has become influential in Jacobin circles. He was among the first to call for an end to the monarchy and adoption of a republic

Robespierre (ROBES-PEE-air). Maximilien Robespierre, 33, was born in Arras (Artois province), far to the north of France near the border with the Austrian Netherlands. Robespierre was largely raised by relatives after the death of his mother—and the frequent absences of his father, a lawyer. He received a scholarship to study at Louis-le-Grand in Paris, where he distinguished himself academically. At 23, he became a lawyer and was admitted to the bar at Arras, where he was elected as a representative for the Third Estate. At Versailles, he endorsed its transformation of the Third Estate into the National Assembly, where he became an ardent apostle of Rousseau—and a leader of the Jacobins.

David (DAH-veed). Jacques-Louis David, 43, successful artist and member of the Royal Academy of Arts, was famous for several prizewinning historical paintings, including the revolutionary *Brutus and the Lictors* (1787). He joined the Jacobin Club, and, in 1790, proposed that the National Assembly replace the Royal Academy of Arts with a Commune of the Arts, freeing art from royal supervision and interference. The National Assembly commissioned him to do a painting depicting the Tennis Court Oath.

Section Leaders of Paris/the Crowd

The people of Paris, guided by the leaders of each of the city's forty-eight sections, have played a major role in the revolution. The king could not crush the National Assembly in July 1789 while tens of thousands of members of the Parisian crowd barred the way of the royalist troops. And it was the Crowd, guided by the leaders of the Commune, who found arms at the *Invalides* and gunpowder at the Bastille. The march to Versailles was, of course, undertaken chiefly by the women of the crowd. Probably a half million Parisians, the overwhelming majority, are small shopkeepers, street vendors, craftsmen, journeymen, laborers, vagrants, and city poor (or the families of same); these people are now known as *sans-culottes* (literally "without knee breeches") because they wear trousers rather than breeches with high silk stockings. There are a handful of textile factories that employ as many as 800 workers each, but most of the artisanal workers—stocking weavers, dyers, glassmakers, building tradesmen, upholsterers, and the like—are employed in small workshops. [For the purposes of the game, the Crowd refers to the *sans-culottes* of Paris, but most of the smaller cities of France experienced dynamics similar to what transpired in the capital.] The section leaders endorse Rousseau's conception of a participatory democracy. They have less use for the National Assembly, a representative body.

Danton [DAN-tawn]. Georges Jacques Danton, 32, born in rural Champagne, the son of a minor clerk, was sent to a seminary at 14. Disinterested in religion, he acquired a law degree in Paris and practiced law there, for a time as "Counsel to the King's Bench." A resident of the Cordeliers section of Paris, he became a leather-lunged orator at the Cordeliers Club. He then organized the people of the section into the Cordeliers Battalion, which participated in several major revolutionary actions, including the procession of the market women to Versailles and the defense of Marat, after the National Assembly had ordered his arrest. In a recent speech at the National Assembly, Danton, though not a member, declared that the king's flight from Paris was part of "a gigantic conspiracy." Danton denounced Lafayette as "either a traitor" or "a plain fool."

Andalle (ann-DAHL). Anne-Marguerite Andall, 41, a linen worker and widow of Joseph François Ravet, lives in the Saint Denis section of Paris. When bakers raised the price of a four-pound loaf of bread from 8 *sous* to 16 *sous* in 1789, she led the women of Saint Denis in storming nearly all of the local bakeries, forcing the bakers to lower prices. She also mobilized the women of the section in the October 1789 march to Versailles, bringing the king and his family back to Paris. She now speaks regularly at the Cordeliers Club.

Hébert (AY-bear). Jean-Paul Hébert, 55, journalist, was born in a town in Normandy, the son of a jeweler and city official. His journalism career attracted attention in 1790 when he lampooned Abbé Maury, a conservative Catholic deputy in the National Assembly. Later that same year, catapulted by his amplified reputation, Hébert founded the *Father Duchesne*, a satirical denunciation of the Ancien Régime liberally sprinkled with coarse expletives.

Léon (LAY-ohn). Pauline Léon, 23, the daughter of a chocolate maker, participated in the rising in Paris on July 14, 1789, chiefly by throwing up barricades to prevent the king's soldiers from attacking the revolutionaries. She also joined in attacks on houses in well-to-do districts, looking for anti-revolutionary traitors. A frequent speaker at the Cordeliers Club, she demands that women be given equal rights— and even allowed into the armed forces. She has already devised a plan to mobilize women revolutionaries to fight in defense of the nation.

Marat (mah-RAH). Jean-Paul Marat, 48, was born in Neuchatel, now a part of Switzerland, but in his teens made his way to Bordeaux and then Paris, where he wrote books on medicine, literature, philosophy, and natural science. In 1774, while practicing medicine in London, he published *The Chains of Slavery*, which advocated violent revolution against tyrannical kings and clerics. In 1789, on the eve of the Estates General, Marat returned to France and published two tracts against the monarchy, which the royal censors banned as sedition. Within a few months he began publishing a newspaper, *The Friend of the People,* which many regard as the voice of violent opposition to injustice.

Rolin (ROW-lawn). Françoise Rolin, 22, was born in Paris and has lived there her whole life. An unmarried florist, she lives in the Saint-Antoine section, one of the city's poorest. When bakers withheld bread in 1789, raising the price, she participated in the riots that forced them to lower prices. She also participated in the march to Versailles, which forced the royal family back to Paris. A striking figure who dresses in red, Rolin has advocated that women be given weapons to assist in defending Paris from foreign invaders—and royalist counterrevolutionaries.

Varlet (Vahr-LAY). Jean-François Varlet, 27, was born and raised in Paris by a widowed mother. She owned some property and Varlet enrolled at the College d'Harcourt, where he became an apostle of Rousseau. In 1790, while attending the celebration marking the first anniversary of the Fall of the Bastille (Festival of the Federation), he attracted attention by giving speeches at the Jacobin Club, the Cordeliers Club, and the Fraternal Society of Both Sexes. He can be seen carrying around a portable podium, along with costumes to attract attention. He especially denounces Lafayette for betraying the Revolution by using the National Guard against the revolutionaries.

[Gracchus] Babeuf (Bah-BOOF). François-Noel (Gracchus) Babeuf, 31, was born to a poor family in a town north of Paris. Though his father did only menial work, he taught François-Noel to read and write. At 22, François-Noel married the daughter of an ironmonger and had a child shortly thereafter. He worked as a land surveyor, but in 1789 became swept up in the revolutionary movement. He published articles denouncing the king and his ministers and was repeatedly arrested. He continues to agitate against the king.

Indeterminates

Most of these are members of the National Assembly.

Hutteau (hoot-TOE). François Louis Hutteau, 62, is a lawyer who was born and raised in Paris. Upon reading *Letters from an American Farmer* by Hector St. John de Crèvecoeur, a Frenchman's illuminating account of life and society in the Americas, Hutteau sold his office and traveled the world in order to write about his experiences, selling his stories to magazines and newspapers. When the king called on the Estates General, Hutteau returned to Paris, was elected to the National Assembly, and has since reported on events in France and elsewhere.

Bouron (BOO-rohn). François Anne Jacques Bouron, 39, a lawyer, was born in the Vendée, far to the west of Paris. He served as a lawyer for the king. He was elected to the Third Estate for the Vendée in 1789 and supported its becoming the National Assembly.

Verny (VAIR-knee). Thomas Verny, 44, a lawyer from Montpellier in the south of France, has attracted notice as a writer and essayist. He is a member of the Academy of Floral Games, the oldest literary society in Europe. (Bertrand Barère, another deputy of the National Assembly, is also a member of the Academy.) Verny, elected to represent Montpellier for the Third Estate, has persuaded the Academy to give an award for the finest essays and speeches on political thought. The Academy recently announced that Verny has been chosen to chair the prize selection committee.

Alquier (al-KEE-ay). Jean-Baptiste Alquier, 40, grew up in La Rochelle, a port on the west coast of France, where he worked as a tax lawyer and adviser to the intendant (the royal administrator). In 1789 he was elected to the Third Estate for La Rochelle. When Louis XVI dismissed Necker as finance minister, Alquier expressed his disappointment. With the formation of the National Assembly, Alquier was appointed to the Committee on Finances, where he has established a reputation as a leading figure on budgetary and economic matters.

Palm (PALM). Etta Palm d'Aelders, 48, was born in Groningen in the Dutch Republic, the daughter of a paper mill owner. Her first marriage was brief; her second marriage, to a well-to-do Dutch patriot, brought her to Paris, where she fell ill. Her husband moved away from Paris but she remained, calling herself the "Baronness d'Aelders." She helped found the Social Circle, an important political club and one of the first to admit women on an equal standing with men. She has cultivated friendships with many of the leading figures in both the court and the revolutionary government. Her *Discourse on the Injustice of the Laws in Favor of Men* was read to the National Assembly last December.

Périer (pay-REE-ay). Claude Périer, 42, was born in Grenoble, the son of a wealthy textile manufacturer. Claude was educated to become a lawyer, though he is interested in Enlightenment thinkers and Rousseau. His wife is a devout Catholic. In 1780 he acquired the chateau of Vizille, which made him a feudal lord; he converted the building, however, into a textile factory. Some have accused him of being a "greedy bourgeois." Yet he supported the mob action that forced the Estates in Grenoble to meet as one, and even proposed that they meet in his chateau. He also supported the Chapelier Law, recently passed, which banned guilds and trade unions. He is a member of the National Assembly.

Polverel (Pole-vair-ell). Charles Polverel, 39, was born in the Americas, where he became famous as a surgeon. In the 1780s, he moved to Paris, set up practice, and became first-surgeon of the Paris Hotel-Dieu hospital. He was swiftly admitted to the Academy of Surgery, and was elected to the Third Estate by virtue of his medical reputation. He has spoken on various matters before the National Assembly, to which he belongs.

Blampain (BLAM-pah). Jean Blampain, 42, a lawyer, was born in Nancy, in northeast France. He attracted a wide following in Nancy, conducting his business of writing wills and marriage contracts, handling land sales, and resolving disputes over wages and contracts from a wine shop. In 1789 he was elected to the Third Estate for Nancy. He was famous for his evenhanded dealings with everyone, rich and poor. He remains a member of the National Assembly.

Lucy (lew-SEE). Etienne Lucy, 39, a lawyer, was born and raised in Paris but also owns farmland in the countryside. For his speeches on Rousseau and ancient history, especially ancient Sparta and Rome, he acquired a reputation as a writer and philosopher. He attends many different political clubs. Unlike most speakers, Lucy often rises to the podium to ask questions rather than answer them. He belongs to the National Assembly.

Dupré (dew-PRAY). Jean Guineau Dupré, 44, a lawyer, was born in Limoges, in southern France. He worked as an attorney on cases before the local courts. He was elected to the Third Estate and became a member of the National Assembly, where he can usually be found in the middle section. He is known for being thoughtful and judicious.

PART 5: **CORE TEXTS**

CHARLES DE SECONDAT, THE BARON DE MONTESQUIEU

Louis XIV and the Critique of Absolutism, 1721

FROM *The Persian Letters*

Montesquieu (1689–1755) was a nobleman, a judge in a French court, and a highly influential political thinker, but his public reputation only began with the publication of The Persian Letters *(1721). Louis XIV had been dead for six years when the novel was published, but it still spent much time and effort criticizing and ridiculing absolutism. This selection mocks French society but does so in the context of an attack on despotism, or the wielding of arbitrary and cruel power by the reigning monarch. You may wish to consider why the critiques of the late king's style of rule are so sharp. Why might Montesquieu have continued to criticize absolutism, even after the Sun King was dead? What are his criticisms? Do these denunciations of absolute power have relevance years later, in the time of Louis XVI?*

SOURCE: *Merrick Whitcomb, ed.,* Translations and Reprints from the Original Sources of European History, *vol. VI (Philadelphia: University of Pennsylvania, 1900), 2–3.*

LETTER XXXVII

Usbek to Ibben in Smyrna.

The king of France is an old man. We have no instance in our history of a monarch that has reigned so long. They say he possesses to an extraordinary degree the talent of making himself obeyed. He governs with the same ability his family, his court, his state. He has often been heard to say that of all the governments of the world, that of the Turks or that of our own august sultan pleased him most, so greatly he affected the oriental style of politics.

I have made a study of his character, and I find contradictions which I am unable to reconcile: for example, he has a minister who is only eighteen years old, and a mistress who is eighty; he is devoted to religion, and he cannot endure those who say it must be rigorously observed; although he flees the tumult of the city and has intercourse [interactions] with few, yet he is occupied from morning until night in making himself talked about; he loves trophies and victories, but he is afraid of seeing a good general at the head of his troops, lest he should have cause to fear the chief of a hostile army.[1] He is the only one, I believe, to whom it has ever happened that he was at the same time overwhelmed with more riches than a prince might hope to possess and burdened with a poverty that a private person would be unable to bear.

He loves to gratify those that serve him; but he rewards the efforts, or rather the indolence, of his courtiers more liberally than the arduous campaigns of his captains. Often he prefers a man whose duty it is to disrobe him or hand him his napkin when he seats himself at dinner, to another who takes cities or wins him battles. He believes that the sovereign grandeur ought not to be limited in the distribution of favors; and without investigating as to whether the one upon whom he heaps benefits is a man of merit, he believes that his choice renders him such; so that he has been seen to give a small pension to a man who had run two leagues, and a fine government to another who had run four.

He is magnificent, especially in his buildings. There are more statues in the gardens of his palace than there are citizens in a great city. His guard is as strong as that of the prince before whom all thrones are overturned; his armies are as numerous, his resources are as great and his finances as inexhaustible.

Paris, the 7th of the moon of Maharram, 1713.

---

1. Louis XIV did have a minister, Barbezieux, who held office at the age of twenty-three— though this man was not actually alive in 1713, when this letter was supposedly written. Louis' mistress (and secret wife), Madame de Maintenon, was indeed older than he was by a few years. This would have made her nearly eighty, as Montesquieu suggests, and she wielded much influence over Louis. When compared to the behavior of a sultan or "Oriental despot," the French king's actions may have seemed no less unpredictable.

CHARLES DE SECONDAT, THE BARON DE MONTESQUIEU

Montesquieu on Government and Liberty, 1748

FROM *The Spirit of the Laws*

Montesquieu presented his sociological and historical research in The Spirit of the Laws, *which is best known for its enunciation of the idea of separation of powers. In this selection, Montesquieu discusses the meaning of liberty, checks and balances, and the significance of both for the English Constitution, which he sees as a nearly ideal example of the preservation of liberty. As you read, you should particularly note Montesquieu's rationale for checks and balances. What happens when the head of state or the nobles have access to excessive power? Compare Montesquieu's idea about the people's ability to govern with what you know about Rousseau's sentiments. What are their similarities and differences?*

SOURCE: *Baron de Montesquieu,* The Spirit of Laws, *trans. Thomas Nugent, vol. 1, (New York: Colonial Press, 1900), 150–158.*

3.—IN WHAT LIBERTY CONSISTS

*I*t is true that in democracies the people seem to act as they please; but political liberty does not consist in an unlimited freedom. In governments, that is, in societies directed by laws, liberty can consist only in the power of doing what we ought to will, and in not being constrained to do what we ought not to will.

We must have continually present to our minds the difference between independence and liberty. Liberty is a right of doing whatever the laws permit, and if a citizen could do what they forbid he would be no longer possessed of liberty, because all his fellow-citizens would have the same power.

4.—THE SAME SUBJECT CONTINUED

Democratic and aristocratic states are not in their own nature free. Political liberty is to be found only in moderate governments; and even in these it is not always found. It is there only when there is no abuse of power. But constant experience shows us that every man invested with power is apt to abuse it, and to carry his authority as far as it will go. Is it not strange, though true, to say that virtue itself has need of limits?

Note that Montesquieu concerns himself not with absolute freedom—independence—but with the relationship between liberty and virtue.

To prevent this abuse, it is necessary from the very nature of things that power should be a check to power. A government may be so constituted, as no man shall be compelled to do things to which the law does not oblige him, nor forced to abstain from things which the law permits.

5.—OF THE END OR VIEW OF DIFFERENT GOVERNMENTS

* * *

One nation there is also in the world that has for the direct end of its constitution political liberty. We shall presently examine the principles on which this liberty is founded; if they are sound, liberty will appear in its highest perfection.

To discover political liberty in a constitution, no great labor is requisite. If we are capable of seeing it where it exists, it is soon found, and we need not go far in search of it.

6.—OF THE CONSTITUTION OF ENGLAND

In every government there are three sorts of power: the legislative; the executive in respect to things dependent on the law of nations; and the executive in regard to matters that depend on the civil law.[1]

By virtue of the first, the prince or magistrate enacts temporary or perpetual laws, and amends or abrogates those that have been already enacted. By the second, he makes peace or war, sends or receives embassies, establishes the public security, and provides against invasions. By the third, he punishes criminals, or determines the disputes that arise between individuals. The latter we shall call the judiciary power, and the other simply the executive power of the state.

The political liberty of the subject is a tranquillity of mind arising from the opinion each person has of his safety. In order to have this liberty, it is requisite the government be so constituted as one man need not be afraid of another.

When the legislative and executive powers are united in the same person, or in the same body of magistrates, there can be no liberty; because apprehensions may arise, lest the same monarch or senate should enact tyrannical laws, to execute them in a tyrannical manner.

Again, there is no liberty, if the judiciary power be not separated from the legislative and executive. Were it joined with the legislative, the life and liberty of the subject would be exposed to arbitrary control; for the judge would be then the legislator. Were it joined to the executive power, the judge might behave with violence and oppression.

Absolute monarchs are not the only ones who can act tyrannically. Unlimited power of any kind will ultimately destroy liberty.

There would be an end of everything, were the same man or the same body, whether of the nobles or of the people, to exercise those three powers, that of enacting laws, that of executing the public resolutions, and of trying the causes of individuals.

* * *

If the legislature leaves the executive power in possession of a right to imprison those subjects who can give security for their good behavior, there is an end of liberty; unless they are taken up, in order to answer without delay to a capital crime, in which case they are really free, being subject only to the power of the law.

Here Montesquieu notes that liberty and threats to the state exist in tension with one another.

But should the legislature think itself in danger by some secret conspiracy against the state, or by a correspondence with a foreign enemy, it might authorize the executive power, for a short and limited time, to imprison suspected persons, who in that case would lose their liberty only for a while, to preserve it forever.

* * *

As in a country of liberty, every man who is supposed a free agent ought to be his own governor; the legislative power should reside in the whole body of the

---

1. "We call these "legislative, executive, and judicial powers."

people. But since this is impossible in large states, and in small ones is subject to many inconveniences, it is fit the people should transact by their representatives what they cannot transact by themselves.

The inhabitants of a particular town are much better acquainted with its wants and interests than with those of other places; and are better judges of the capacity of their neighbors than of that of the rest of their countrymen. The members, therefore, of the legislature should not be chosen from the general body of the nation; but it is proper that in every considerable place a representative should be elected by the inhabitants.

The great advantage of representatives is, their capacity of discussing public affairs. For this the people collectively are extremely unfit, which is one of the chief inconveniences of a democracy.

* * *

In such a state there are always persons distinguished by their birth, riches, or honors: but were they to be confounded with the common people, and to have only the weight of a single vote like the rest, the common liberty would be their slavery, and they would have no interest in supporting it, as most of the popular resolutions would be against them. The share they have, therefore, in the legislature ought to be proportioned to their other advantages in the state; which happens only when they form a body that has a right to check the licentiousness of the people, as the people have a right to oppose any encroachment of theirs.

The legislative power is therefore committed to the body of the nobles, and to that which represents the people, each having their assemblies and deliberations apart, each their separate views and interests.

Of the three powers above mentioned, the judiciary is in some measure next to nothing: there remain, therefore, only two; and as these have need of a regulating power to moderate them, the part of the legislative body composed of the nobility is extremely proper for this purpose.

The body of the nobility ought to be hereditary. In the first place it is so in its own nature; and in the next there must be a considerable interest to preserve its privileges—privileges that in themselves are obnoxious to popular envy, and of course in a free state are always in danger.

But as a hereditary power might be tempted to pursue its own particular interests, and forget those of the people, it is proper that where a singular advantage may be gained by corrupting the nobility, as in the laws relating to the supplies, they should have no other share in the legislation than the power of rejecting, and not that of resolving.

By the power of resolving I mean the right of ordaining by their own authority, or of amending what has been ordained by others. By the power of rejecting I would be understood to mean the right of annulling a resolution taken by another; which was the power of the tribunes at Rome. And though the person possessed of the privilege of rejecting may likewise have the right of approving, yet this approbation passes for no more than a declaration, that he intends to make no use of his privilege of rejecting, and is derived from that very privilege.

Government laws must be carried out rationally and quickly; this is most likely to happen when the executive power is found in a single person.

The executive power ought to be in the hands of a monarch, because this branch of government, having need of despatch, is better administered by one than by many: on the other hand, whatever depends on the legislative power is oftentimes better regulated by many than by a single person.

But if there were no monarch, and the executive power should be committed to a certain number of persons selected from the legislative body, there would be an end then of liberty; by reason the two powers would be united, as the same persons would sometimes possess, and would be always able to possess, a share in both.

Were the legislative body to be a considerable time without meeting, this would likewise put an end to liberty. For of two things one would naturally follow: either that there would be no longer any legislative resolutions, and then the state would fall into anarchy; or that these resolutions would be taken by the executive power, which would render it absolute.

It would be needless for the legislative body to continue always assembled. This would be troublesome to the representatives, and, moreover, would cut out too much work for the executive power, so as to take off its attention to its office, and oblige it to think only of defending its own prerogatives, and the right it has to execute.

Again, were the legislative body to be always assembled, it might happen to be kept up only by filling the places of the deceased members with new representatives; and in that case, if the legislative body were once corrupted, the evil would be past all remedy. When different legislative bodies succeed one another, the people who have a bad opinion of that which is actually sitting may reasonably entertain some hopes of the next: but were it to be always the same body, the people upon seeing it once corrupted would no longer expect any good from its laws; and of course they would either become desperate or fall into a state of indolence.

The legislative body should not meet of itself. For a body is supposed to have no will but when it is met; and besides, were it not to meet unanimously, it would be impossible to determine which was really the legislative body; the part assembled, or the other. And if it had a right to prorogue itself, it might happen never to be prorogued; which would be extremely dangerous, in case it should ever attempt to encroach on the executive power. Besides, there are seasons, some more proper than others, for assembling the legislative body: it is fit, therefore, that the executive power should regulate the time of meeting, as well as the duration of those assemblies, according to the circumstances and exigencies of a state known to itself.

Were the executive power not to have a right of restraining the encroachments of the legislative body, the latter would become despotic; for as it might arrogate to itself what authority it pleased, it would soon destroy all the other powers.[2]

---

2. Montesquieu worries that a legislature with no executive to check it will become despotic. This argument is particularly important in the legislative debate over the king's veto.

But it is not proper, on the other hand, that the legislative power should have a right to stay the executive. For as the execution has its natural limits, it is useless to confine it; besides, the executive power is generally employed in momentary operations. The power, therefore, of the Roman tribunes was faulty, as it put a stop not only to the legislation, but likewise to the executive part of government; which was attended with infinite mischief.

But if the legislative power in a free state has no right to stay the executive, it has a right and ought to have the means of examining in what manner its laws have been executed; an advantage which this government has over that of Crete and Sparta, where the Cosmi and the Ephori gave no account of their administration.

But whatever may be the issue of that examination, the legislative body ought not to have a power of arraigning the person, nor, of course, the conduct, of him who is intrusted with the executive power. His person should be sacred, because as it is necessary for the good of the state to prevent the legislative body from rendering themselves arbitrary, the moment he is accused or tried there is an end of liberty.

ARTHUR YOUNG

Abuses of the Ancien Régime: Hunting Rights, 1787–1789

FROM *Travels in France during the Years 1787, 1788, 1789*

Arthur Young was a wealthy English farmer who traveled about France in the three years preceding the Revolution, intending to explore France's methods and natural resources. In this passage, Young gives details of specific feudal rights—hunting privileges—that were held for nobles and the royal family. While the rights were abolished with the August Decrees, this document is useful for helping the reader sense the emotional and social impact of feudalism. As you read it, think about how Arthur Young, a foreigner, describes the game preserves (capitaineries), and what impact they had on humans who lived nearby.

SOURCE: *James Harvey Robinson,* Readings in European History, *abr. ed. (Boston: Ginn & Co., 1906), 413–414.*

*T*he *capitaineries* were a dreadful scourge on all the occupiers of land.[1] By this term is to be understood the paramountship of certain districts granted by the king to princes of the blood, by which they were put in possession of the property of all game, even on lands not belonging to them; and what is very singular, on manors granted long before to individuals; so that the erecting of a district into a *capitainerie* was an annihilation of all manorial rights to game within it. This was a trifling business in comparison to other circumstances; for in speaking of the preservation of the game in these *capitaineries* it must be observed that by game must be understood whole droves of wild boars, and herds of deer not confined by any wall or pale, but wandering at pleasure over the whole country, to the destruction of crops, and to the peopling of the galleys by wretched peasants who presumed to kill them in order to save that food which was to support their helpless children.

Here, Young describes some feudal privileges that also came under protest in the cahiers that were produced leading up to the meeting of the Estates-General.

The game in the *capitainerie* of Montceau, in four parishes only, did mischief to the amount of 184,263 *livres* per annum. No wonder then that we should find the people asking, "We loudly demand the destruction of all the *capitaineries* and of all the various kinds of game." And what are we to think of demanding as a favor the permission "to thresh their grain, mow their fields, and take away the stubble without regard to the partridge or other game"? Now an English reader will scarcely understand without being told that there were numerous edicts for preserving the game, which prohibited weeding and hoeing lest the young partridges should be disturbed, steeping seed lest it should injure the game, . . . mowing hay, etc., before a certain time so late as to spoil many crops; and taking away the stubble which would deprive the birds of shelter.

---

1. *Captitaineries* were lands that existed as hunting preserves in France, reserved for the pleasure of particular nobles, even when the land was not owned by them.

VOLTAIRE

Law, Religion, and the State, 1764

FROM *Philosophical Dictionary*

The philosophe François-Marie Arouet, better known by his pen name Voltaire (1694–1778), was extremely committed to the idea of church reform. He argued for the fundamental nature of liberty, including freedom of conscience, and demanded the creation of a state where church power did not influence state functions. Though Voltaire's thought was very radical when it was first published, it came to be seen as common sense by many of the deputies who were influenced by the Enlightenment. As you read the structure and intent of the Civil Constitution of the Clergy (p. 128), some of these ideas will indicate how attempts to formulate limitations on religious power were defended.

SOURCE: *James Harvey Robinson, Readings in European History, abr. ed. (Boston: Ginn & Co., 1906), 423–424.*

No law made by the Church should ever have the least force unless expressly sanctioned by the government. It was owing to this precaution that Athens and Rome escaped all religious quarrels.

Such religious quarrels are the trait of barbarous nations or such as have become barbarous.

The civil magistrate alone may permit or prohibit labor on religious festivals, since it is not the function of the priest to forbid men to cultivate their fields.

Everything relating to marriage should depend entirely upon the civil magistrate. The priests should confine themselves to the august function of blessing the union.

Lending money at interest should be regulated entirely by the civil law, since trade is governed by civil law.

All ecclesiastics should be subject in every case to the government, since they are subjects of the state.

Never should the ridiculous and shameful custom be maintained of paying to a foreign priest the first year's revenue of land given to a priest by his fellow-citizens.

No priest can deprive a citizen of the least of his rights on the ground that the citizen is a sinner, since the priest—himself a sinner—should pray for other sinners, not judge them.

Officials, laborers, and priests should all alike pay the taxes of the state, since they all alike belong to the state.

There should be but one standard of weights and measures and one system of law.

Let the punishment of criminals be useful. A man when hanged is good for nothing: a man condemned to hard labor continues to serve his country and furnish a living lesson.

Every law should be clear, uniform, and precise. To interpret law is almost always to corrupt it.

Nothing should be regarded as infamous except vice.

The taxes should never be otherwise than proportional to the resources of him who pays.

VOLTAIRE

Liberty and Fundamental Laws, 1764

Here, Voltaire uses his classic biting wit to link religious fanaticism and unjust behavior. In this dialogue, conducted between persons referred to as A, B, and C, Voltaire also sets the stage for the argument that religious belief is both irrational and damaging to society.

SOURCE: Translations and Reprints from the Original Sources of European History, *vol. VI* (Philadelphia: University of PA, 1900), 7–9.

CONCERNING FUNDAMENTAL LAWS

B. I have always heard talk of fundamental laws, but is there any such thing?

A. Yes, there is the law of being just; and nothing fundamental was ever more often shaken.

C. I read not long ago one of those very rare bad books, which the curious are always searching for, as naturalists collect fragments of petrified animal and vegetable substances, imagining that in this way they will discover the secret of nature. This book was written by a lawyer of Paris, named Louis Dorleans, who pleaded strongly against Henry IV before the League, and who fortunately lost his suit.[1] See how this jurisconsult expresses himself concerning the fundamental laws of the kingdom of France. "The fundamental law of the Hebrews was that lepers could not reign: Henry IV is a heretic, hence he is leprous, hence he cannot be king of France according to the fundamental law of the Church. The law contemplates that a king of France shall be a Christian as well as a male; whoever holds not to the Catholic faith, Apostolic and Roman, is not a Christian and does not believe in God; he may no more be king of France than the greatest jackanapes in the world," etc.

It is very true that at Rome every man who does not believe in the pope is a disbeliever in God; but that is not so absolutely true in the rest of the world; it is necessary to make some little restriction: and it seems to me that, taking everything into consideration, Master Louis Dorleans, advocate to the Parlement of Paris, did not reason quite so well as Cicero and Demosthenes.

B. It would please me to see what would become of the fundamental law of the Holy Roman Empire, if some day the electors should take a fancy to choose a Protestant Caesar in that charming city of Frankfort-on-Main.

---

1. The Catholic League argued against Henri IV's legitimacy to rule because of his Huguenot (Protestant) past.

A. The same thing would happen which has happened already to the fundamental law that fixes the number of electors at seven, because there are seven heavens, and because the candlestick of a Jewish temple had seven branches.

Is it not a fundamental law in France that the domain of the King is inalienable? How is it then that it is almost wholly alienated? You will say that all these foundations are laid upon shifting sand. The laws which they call fundamental laws are, like all others, nothing more than laws of convention, of ancient usage, of ancient prejudice, which change according to the times. Ask the Romans of to-day if they have preserved the fundamental laws of the ancient Roman republic. It was well that the domains of the kings of England, France, and Spain should remain attached to the crown when the kings lived as you and I, from the product of their lands; but to-day, when they live exclusively from taxes and imposts, what matters it whether they possess the domains or not? When Francis I failed in his promise to Charles V, his conqueror, when in this connection he violated his oath to yield up Burgundy to him, he caused it to be represented by his lawyers that the Burgundians were inalienable; but if Charles V had come to him to make representations to the contrary at the head of a great army, the Burgundians would have been quite alienable.

Voltaire uses both history and rationalism to make his point. What is the fundamental law, according to Voltaire? How does that set a foundation for arguments that deputies, influenced by Enlightenment thought, will use?

Franche-Comté, whose fundamental law was to be free under the house of Austria, is attached to-day in an intimate and essential manner to the crown of France. The Swiss once held materially to the empire, and now hold materially to liberty.

It is this liberty which is the fundamental law of all nations; it is the only law against which there is no proscription, because it is the law of nature. The Romans might say to the pope: our fundamental law at the start was to have a king who reigned over a league of country; then it was to elect two consuls, then two tribunes; then our fundamental law was to be devoured by an emperor, then to be devoured by the peoples come from the north, then to be in a state of anarchy, then to die of hunger under the government of a priest. At length we return to the true fundamental law, which is to be free: go and give elsewhere your indulgences *in articulo mortis*,[2] and go forth from the Capitol, which was not built for you!

B. Amen!

C. You cannot help hoping that the thing will arrive some day. It would be a fine sight for our grandchildren.

A. Would to Heaven that the grandparents might have the pleasure! It is of all revolutions the easiest to bring about; and meanwhile no one thinks of it.

B. It is because, as you have said, the chief characteristic of men is to be sots and poltroons. The Roman rats are not yet knowing enough to bell the cat.[3]

---

2. In *articulo mortis:* At the point of death, at the hour of death.

3. To bell the cat: To offer a warning to all the mice or animals that might be preyed upon by the cat's claws. The idiom, which comes from a fable, also implies carrying out an impossible task, as it was to be done by the mice themselves.

C. Shall we not admit then any fundamental law whatsoever?

A. Liberty embraces all. That the agriculturist should not be vexed by a tyrant's minion; that no citizen should be imprisoned without immediate trial before his natural judges, who shall decide between him and his prosecutor; that no one shall take from a man his meadow or his vineyard, under pretext of the public good, without ample recompense; that they shall seek the people's good, instead of wishing to rule over them in fattening on their substance; that the law, and not caprice shall reign.

C. The human race is ready to endorse all that.

JEAN-JACQUES ROUSSEAU

Nature and Civilization, 1762

FROM *Emile, or On Education*

Here, Jean-Jacques Rousseau (1712–1778) clearly formulates one of his most famous assertions: man is made good and spoiled only by society. The selection, from his educational treatise Emile, or On Education, *published in 1762, influenced a generation of thinkers who came to believe that man must take his cues from nature in order to create a better civilization.*

SOURCE: *James Harvey Robinson,* Readings in European History, *abr. ed. (Boston: Ginn & Co., 1906), 424–426.*

All things are good as their Author made them, but everything degenerates in the hands of man. By man our native soil is forced to nourish plants brought from foreign regions, and one tree is made to bear the fruit of another. Man brings about a general confusion of elements, climates, and seasons; he mutilates his dogs, his horses, and his slaves; he defaces and confounds everything, and seems to delight only in monsters and deformity. He is not content with anything as Nature left it, not even with man, whom he must train for his service like a saddle horse, and twist in his own particular way like a tree in his garden.

Yet without this interference matters would be still worse than they are, for our species cannot remain half made over. As things now are, a man left to himself from his birth would, in his association with others, prove the most preposterous creature possible. The prejudices, authority, necessity, and example, and, in short, the vicious social institutions in which we find ourselves submerged, would stifle everything natural in him and yet give him nothing in return. He

Rousseau's thoughts on education suggest that the remaking of society holds unique promise. Think about this argument in the context of legislative reform.

would be like a shrub which has sprung up by accident in the middle of the highway to perish by being thrust this way and that and trampled upon by passers-by. . . .

To form this rare creature, man, what have we to do? Much, doubtless, but chiefly to prevent anything being done. . . . In the natural order of things, all men being equal, their common vocation is manhood, and whoever is well trained for that cannot fulfill any vocation badly which demands manhood. Whether my pupil be destined for the army, the church, or the bar, concerns me but little. Before he is called to the career chosen by his parents, Nature summons him to the duties of human life. To live is the trade I wish to teach him. . . . All our wisdom consists in servile prejudices; all our customs are but suggestion, anxiety, and constraint. Civilized man is born, lives, dies in a state of slavery. At his birth he is sewed in swaddling clothes; at his death he is nailed in a coffin; and as long as he preserves the human form he is fettered by our institutions. It is said that nurses sometimes claim to give the infant's head a better form by kneading it, and we permit them to do this! It would appear that our heads were badly fashioned by the Author of Nature, and that they need to be made over outwardly by the midwife and inwardly by philosophers! The Caribbeans are more fortunate than we by half. . . . Observe Nature and follow the path she traces for you!

JEAN-JACQUES ROUSSEAU

FROM *First Discourse: On the Moral Effects of the Arts and Sciences*, 1750

This version of Jean-Jacques Rousseau's First Discourse *has been edited, reorganized, and abridged for this game book. Some of the original footnotes have been omitted. Originally, Rousseau submitted this essay for a competition sponsored by the Academy of Dijon. The Academy proposed this question: "Has the restoration of arts and sciences had a purifying effect upon morals?" Rousseau's response was, as he knew, unexpected for his readers. Instead of answering in the affirmative, Rousseau insisted that greater attention to arts and sciences had damaged morality— that knowledge and learning made men worse rather than helping them improve. His argument contradicted the assumptions of many of the other* philosophes *about the source and meaning of virtue. As you read this essay, think about its application to questions about what society's priorities should be and who is most suited to govern.*

SOURCE: *Jean Jacques Rousseau,* Social Contract & Discourses. *New York: E. P. Dutton & Co., 1913. Translated by G. D. H. Cole (1915).*

PREFACE

*T*he question before me is: "Whether the Restoration of the arts and sciences has had the effect of purifying or corrupting morals." Which side am I to take?

I feel the difficulty of treating this subject fittingly, before the tribunal which is to judge of what I advance. How can I presume to belittle the sciences before one of the most learned assemblies in Europe, to commend ignorance in a famous Academy, and reconcile my contempt for study with the respect due to the truly learned? I was aware of these inconsistencies, but not discouraged by them. It is not science, I said to myself, that I am attacking; it is virtue that I am defending, and that before virtuous men—and goodness is ever dearer to the good than learning to the learned. . . . I have upheld the cause of truth to the best of my natural abilities, whatever my apparent success, there is one reward which cannot fail me. That reward I shall find in the bottom of my heart.

Rousseau hopes that the distinguished professors at the Dijon Academy are men of virtue who will be open to the idea that learning damages morals. Even if they are not, he must write for the sake of truth.

PART I

It is a noble and beautiful spectacle to see man raising himself, so to speak, from nothing by his own exertions; dissipating, by the light of reason, all the thick clouds in which he was by nature enveloped; mounting above himself; soaring in thought even to the celestial regions; like the sun, encompassing with giant strides the vast extent of the universe; and, what is still grander and more wonderful, going back into himself, there to study man and get to know his own nature, his duties and his end. All these miracles we have seen renewed within the last few generations.

Rousseau alludes to the advances of the Enlightenment— new scientific discoveries, the diffusion of knowledge by means of the printing press, and numerous advances in music, art, literature, and the theater, including those works celebrated by a philosophically-inclined public.

* * *

The mind, as well as the body, has its needs: those of the body are the basis of society, those of the mind its ornaments.

So long as government and law provide for the security and well-being of men in their common life, the arts, literature, and the sciences, less despotic though perhaps more powerful, fling garlands of flowers over the chains which weigh them down. They stifle in men's breasts that sense of original liberty, for which they seem to have been born; cause them to love their own slavery, and so make of them what is called a civilized people. Necessity raised up thrones; the arts and sciences have made them strong. Powers of the earth, cherish all talents and protect those who cultivate them. Civilized peoples, cultivate such pursuits: to them, happy slaves, you owe that delicacy and exquisiteness of taste, which is so much your boast, that sweetness of disposition and

Governments became more powerful even as art and literature became more attractive and widespread. Rousseau claims that these worked together to make men "civilized," but this civilization was a form of slavery, with only the appearance of virtue.

urbanity of manners which make intercourse so easy and agreeable among you—in a word, the appearance of all the virtues, without being in possession of one of them.

* * *

What happiness would it be for those who live among us, if our external appearance were always a true mirror of our hearts; if decorum were but virtue; if the maxims we professed were the rules of our conduct; and if real philosophy were inseparable from the title of a philosopher! But so many good qualities too seldom go together; virtue rarely appears in so much pomp and state. Richness of apparel may proclaim the man of fortune, and elegance the man of taste; but true health and manliness are known by different signs. It is under the homespun of the laborer, and not beneath the gilt and tinsel of the courtier, that we should look for strength and vigour of body. External ornaments are no less foreign to virtue, which is the strength and activity of the mind. The honest man is an athlete, who loves to wrestle stark naked; he scorns all those vile trappings, which prevent the exertion of his strength, and were, for the most part, invented only to conceal some deformity.

Before art had molded our behavior [or, more precisely, our manners and customs], and taught our passions to speak an artificial language, our morals were rude but natural; and the different ways in which we behaved proclaimed at the first glance the difference of our dispositions. Human nature was not at bottom better then than now; but men found their security in the ease with which they could see through one another, and this advantage, of which we no longer feel the value, prevented their having many vices.

This is the underlying theme of much of this essay. The less educated man is more truthful. He is a man who doesn't know enough to conceal how he feels, who merely behaves honestly, and he is therefore the ideal citizen.

Nowadays, when more subtle study and a more refined taste have reduced the art of pleasing to a system, there prevails in modern manners a servile and deceptive conformity; so that one would think every mind had been cast in the same mold. Politeness requires this thing; decorum that; ceremony has its forms, and fashion its laws, and these we must always follow, never the promptings of our own nature. We no longer dare seem what we really are, but lie under a perpetual restraint; in the meantime the herd of men, which we call society, all act under the same circumstances exactly alike, unless very particular and powerful motives prevent them. Thus we never know with whom we have to deal; and even to know our friends we must wait for some critical and pressing occasion; that is, till it is too late; for it is on those very occasions that such knowledge is of use to us.

We are civilized but false. Our education has taught us to pretend to be what we are not. Because we are exceedingly polite, our society seems moral, but this is a fiction.

* * *

Where there is no effect, it is idle to look for a cause: but here the effect is certain and the depravity actual; our minds have been corrupted in proportion as the arts and sciences have improved.

* * *

Contrast with [numerous historical] instances the morals of those few nations which, being preserved from the contagion of useless knowledge, have by their virtues become happy in themselves and afforded an example to the rest of the world. . . . [Many peoples] have preferred other activities to those of the mind. They were not ignorant that in other countries there were men who spent their time in disputing idly about the sovereign good, and about vice and virtue. They knew that these useless thinkers were lavish in their own praises, and stigmatized other nations contemptuously as barbarians. But they noted the morals of these people, and so learnt what to think of their learning.

Rousseau outlines why Sparta is better than Athens: Spartan militarism, simplicity, and virtue is better than Athenian glory, prosperity, arts, and cleverness, both in war (Sparta defeated Athens in the Peloponnesian War) and philosophically (he gives the example of Socrates).

Can it be forgotten that, in the very heart of Greece, there arose a city as famous for the happy ignorance of its inhabitants, as for the wisdom of its laws; a republic of demigods rather than of men, so greatly superior their virtues seemed to those of mere humanity? Sparta, eternal proof of the vanity of science, while the vices, under the conduct of the fine arts, were being introduced into Athens, even while its tyrant was carefully collecting together the works of the prince of poets, was driving from her walls artists and the arts, the learned and their learning!

The difference was seen in the outcome. Athens became the seat of politeness and taste, the country of orators and philosophers. The elegance of its buildings equalled that of its language; on every side might be seen marble and canvas, animated by the hands of the most skilled artists. From Athens we derive those astonishing performances, which will serve as models to every corrupt age.

The picture of Lacedaemon [Sparta] is not so highly colored. There, the neighboring nations used to say, "men were born virtuous, their native air seeming to inspire them with virtue." But its inhabitants have left us nothing but the memory of their heroic actions: monuments that should not count for less in our eyes than the most curious relics of Athenian marble.

It is true that, among the Athenians, there were some few wise men who withstood the general torrent, and preserved their integrity even in the company of the Muses. But hear the judgment which Socrates, the greatest—and most unhappy—of them, passed on the artists and learned men of his day. "I have considered the poets," says he, "and I look upon them as people whose talents impose both on themselves and on others; they give themselves out for wise men, and are taken for such; but in reality they are anything sooner than that."

"From the poets," continues Socrates, "I turned to the artists. Nobody was more ignorant of the arts than myself; nobody was more fully persuaded that the artists were possessed of amazing knowledge. I soon discovered, however, that they were in as bad a way as the poets, and that both had fallen into the same misconception. Because the most skillful of them excel others in their particular jobs, they think themselves wiser than all the rest of mankind. This arrogance spoilt all their skill in my eyes, so that, putting myself in the place of the oracle, and asking myself whether I would rather be what I am or what they are, know what they know, or know that I know nothing, I very readily answered, for myself and the god, that I had rather remain as I am.

"None of us, neither the sophists, nor the poets, nor the orators, nor the artists, nor I, know what is the nature of the true, the good, or the beautiful. But there is this difference between us; that, though none of these people know anything, they all think they know something; whereas for my part, if I know nothing, I am at least in no doubt of my ignorance. So the superiority of wisdom, imputed to me by the oracle, is reduced merely to my being fully convinced that I am ignorant of what I do not know."

Thus we find Socrates, the wisest of men in the judgment of the gods, and the most learned of all the Athenians in the opinion of all Greece, speaking in praise of ignorance. Were he alive now, there is little reason to think that our modern scholars and artists would induce him to change his mind. No, gentlemen, that honest man would still persist in despising our vain sciences. He would lend no aid to swell the flood of books that flows from every quarter: he would leave to us, as he did to his disciples, only the example and memory of his virtues; that is the noblest method of instructing mankind.

* * *

But let pass the distance of time and place, and let us see what has happened in our own time and country; or rather let us banish odious descriptions that might offend our delicacy, and spare ourselves the pains of repeating the same things under different names. . . . It is true that in France Socrates would not have drunk the hemlock, but he would have drunk of a potion infinitely more bitter, of insult, mockery, and contempt a hundred times worse than death. Thus it is that luxury, profligacy, and slavery have been, in all ages, the scourge of the efforts of our pride to emerge from that happy state of ignorance, in which the wisdom of providence had placed us. That thick veil with which it has covered all its operations seems to be a sufficient proof that it never designed us for such fruitless researches. But is there, indeed, one lesson it has taught us, by which we have rightly profited, or which we have neglected with impunity?

Rousseau again takes a different path from other philosophes. He argues that rationality does not offer access to all truth, nor ought it. Rather, nature protects men from themselves by hiding her secrets, by making knowledge difficult to acquire.

Let men learn for once that nature would have preserved them from science, as a mother snatches a dangerous weapon from the hands of her child. Let them know that all the secrets she hides are so many evils from which she protects them, and that the very difficulty they find in acquiring knowledge is not the least of her bounty towards them. Men are perverse; but they would have been far worse, if they had had the misfortune to be born learned.

How humiliating are these reflections to humanity, and how mortified by them our pride should be! What! it will be asked, is uprightness the child of ignorance? Is virtue inconsistent with learning? What consequences might not be drawn from such suppositions? But to reconcile these apparent contradictions, we need only examine closely the emptiness and vanity of those pompous titles, which are so liberally bestowed on human knowledge, and which so blind our judgment. Let us consider, therefore, the arts and sciences in themselves. Let us see what must result from their advancement, and let us not hesitate to admit the truth of all those points on which our arguments coincide with the inductions we can make from history.

PART II

In the past, when society was closer to truth, people knew that the arts and sciences had emerged from evil, and they communicated that story of the origins of knowledge in their myths. Knowledge arose from human vice.

An ancient tradition passed out of Egypt into Greece, that some god, who was an enemy to the repose of mankind, was the inventor of the sciences. What must the Egyptians, among whom the sciences first arose, have thought of them? And they beheld, near at hand, the sources from which they sprang. In fact, whether we turn to the annals of the world, or eke out with philosophical investigations the uncertain chronicles of history, we shall not find for human knowledge an origin answering to the idea we are pleased to entertain of it at present. Astronomy was born of superstition, eloquence of ambition, hatred, falsehood, and flattery; geometry of avarice; physics of an idle curiosity; and even moral philosophy of human pride. Thus the arts and sciences owe their birth to our vices; we should be less doubtful of their advantages, if they had sprung from our virtues.

* * *

Those who become educated produce nothing and instead spend their lives in pointless debates over useless matters. Further, the learned oppose contemporary values and thus seek to destroy all the values that support society: patriotism, virtue, religion.

If our sciences are futile in the objects they propose, they are no less dangerous in the effects they produce. Being the effect of idleness, they generate idleness in their turn; and an irreparable loss of time is the first prejudice which they must necessarily cause to society. To live without doing some good is a great evil as well in the political as in the moral world; and hence every useless citizen should be regarded as a pernicious person. Tell me then, illustrious philosophers, of whom we learn the ratios in which attraction acts in vacuo; and in the revolution of the planets, the relations of spaces traversed in equal times; by whom we are taught what curves have conjugate points, points of inflexion, and cusps; how the soul and body correspond, like two clocks, without actual communication; what planets may be inhabited; and what insects reproduce in an extraordinary manner. Answer me, I say, you from whom we receive all this sublime information, whether we should have been less numerous, worse governed, less formidable, less flourishing, or more perverse, supposing you had taught us none of all these fine things. Reconsider therefore the importance of your productions; and, since the labors of the most enlightened of our learned men and the best of our citizens are of so little utility, tell us what we ought to think of that numerous herd of obscure writers and useless litterateurs, who devour without any return the substance of the State.

Useless, do I say? Would God they were! Society would be more peaceful, and morals less corrupt. But these vain and futile declaimers go forth on all sides, armed with their fatal paradoxes, to sap the foundations of our faith, and nullify virtue. They smile contemptuously at such old names as patriotism and religion, and consecrate their talents and philosophy to the destruction and defamation of all that men hold sacred. Not that they bear any real hatred to virtue or dogma; they are the enemies of public opinion alone; to bring them to the foot of the altar, it would be enough to banish them to a land of atheists. What extravagancies will not the rage of singularity induce men to commit!

* * *

We cannot reflect on the morality of mankind without contemplating with pleasure the picture of the simplicity which prevailed in the earliest times. This image may be justly compared to a beautiful coast, adorned only by the hands of nature; towards which our eyes are constantly turned, and which we see receding with regret. While men were innocent and virtuous and loved to have the gods for witnesses of their actions, they dwelt together in the same huts; but when they became vicious, they grew tired of such inconvenient onlookers, and banished them to magnificent temples. Finally, they expelled their deities even from these, in order to dwell there themselves; or at least the temples of the gods were no longer more magnificent than the palaces of the citizens. This was the height of degeneracy; nor could vice ever be carried to greater lengths than when it was seen, supported, as it were, at the doors of the great, on columns of marble, and graven on Corinthian capitals. As the conveniences of life increase, as the arts are brought to perfection, and luxury spreads, true courage flags, the virtues disappear; and all this is the effect of the sciences and of those acts which are exercised in the privacy of men's dwellings.

What role does Rousseau imply that religion should have in public life? How does this relate to luxury, citizenship, and everyday existence?

When the Goths ravaged Greece, the libraries only escaped the flames owing to an opinion that was set on foot among them, that it was best to leave the enemy with a possession so calculated to divert their attention from military exercises, and keep them engaged in indolent and sedentary occupations. Charles the Eighth found himself master of Tuscany and the kingdom of Naples, almost without drawing sword; and all his court attributed this unexpected success to the fact that the princes and nobles of Italy applied themselves with greater earnestness to the cultivation of their understandings than to active and martial pursuits. In fact, says the sensible person who records these characteristics, experience plainly tells us that in military matters and all that resemble them application to the sciences tends rather to make men effeminate and cowardly than resolute and vigorous.

* * *

If the cultivation of the sciences is prejudicial to military qualities, it is still more so to moral qualities. Even from our infancy an absurd system of education serves to adorn our wit and corrupt our judgment. We see, on every side, huge

The youth of our time demonstrate that they are less virtuous than those who came before. Contemporary society is more inclined to depict bad morals, increasingly tends toward injustice and inequality, and is more likely to reward learning over virtue.

institutions, where our youth are educated at great expense, and instructed in everything but their duty. Your children will be ignorant of their own language, when they can talk others which are not spoken anywhere. They will be able to compose verses which they can hardly understand; and, without being capable of distinguishing truth from error, they will possess the art of making them unrecognizable by specious arguments. But magnanimity, equity, temperance, humanity, and courage will be words of which they know not the meaning. The dear name of country will never strike on their ears; and if they ever hear speak of God, it will be less to fear than to be frightened of Him. I would as soon, said a wise man, that my pupil had spent his time in the tennis court as in this manner; for there his body at least would have got exercise. I well know that children ought to be kept employed, and that idleness is for them the danger most to be feared. But what should they be taught? This is undoubtedly an important question. Let them be taught what they are to practice when they come to be men; not what they ought to forget.

* * *

The question is no longer whether a man is honest, but whether he is clever. We do not ask whether a book is useful, but whether it is well written. Rewards are lavished on wit and ingenuity, while virtue is left unhonored. There are a thousand prizes for fine discourses, and none for good actions. I should be glad, however, to know whether the honor attaching to the best discourse that ever wins the prize in this Academy is comparable with the merit of having founded the prize.

A wise man does not go in chase of fortune; but he is by no means insensible to glory, and when he sees it so ill distributed, his virtue, which might have been animated by a little emulation, and turned to the advantage of society, droops, and dies away in obscurity and indigence. It is for this reason that the agreeable arts must in time everywhere be preferred to the useful; and this truth has been but too much confirmed since the revival of the arts and sciences. We have physicists, geometricians, chemists, astronomers, poets, musicians, and painters in plenty; but we have no longer a citizen among us; or if there be found a few scattered over our abandoned countryside, they are left to perish there unnoticed and neglected. Such is the condition to which we are reduced, and such are our feelings towards those who give us our daily bread, and our children milk.

The wise are particularly culpable, for they court fame and prestige, rather than virtue.

* * *

But if the progress of the arts and sciences has added nothing to our real happiness; if it has corrupted our morals, and if that corruption has vitiated our taste, what are we to think of the herd of textbook authors, who have removed those impediments which nature purposely laid in the way to the Temple of the Muses, in order to guard its approach and try the powers of those who might be tempted to seek knowledge? What are we to think of those compilers who have indiscreetly broken open the door of the sciences, and introduced into their sanctuary a populace unworthy to approach it, when it was greatly to be wished that all who should be found incapable of making a considerable progress in the career of learning should have been repulsed at the entrance, and thereby cast upon those arts which are useful to society. A man who will be all his life a bad versifier, or a third-rate geometrician, might have made nevertheless an excellent clothier. Those whom nature intended for her disciples have not needed masters. Bacon, Descartes, and Newton, those teachers of mankind, had themselves no teachers. What guide indeed could have taken them so far as their sublime genius directed them? Ordinary masters would only have cramped their intelligence, by confining it within the narrow limits of their own capacity. It was from the obstacles they met with at first that they learned to exert themselves, and bestirred themselves to traverse the vast field which they covered. If it be proper to allow some men to apply themselves to the study of the arts and sciences, it is only those who feel themselves able to walk alone in their footsteps and to outstrip them. It belongs only to these few to raise monuments to the glory of the human understanding. But if we are desirous that nothing should be above their genius, nothing should be beyond their hopes. This is the only encouragement they require.

Ultimately, Rousseau argues that real genius needs no teachers and institutions of higher learning rarely advance it.

* * *

As for us, ordinary men, on whom Heaven has not been pleased to bestow such great talents; as we are not destined to reap such glory, let us remain in our obscurity. Let us not covet a reputation we should never attain, and which, in the present state of things, would never make up to us for the trouble it would have cost us, even if we were fully qualified to obtain it. Why should we build our happiness on the opinions of others, when we can find it in our own hearts? Let us leave to others the task of instructing mankind in their duty, and confine ourselves to the discharge of our own. We have no occasion for greater knowledge than this. Virtue! Sublime science of simple minds, are such industry and preparation needed if we are to know you? Are not your principles graven on every heart? Need we do more, to learn your laws, than examine ourselves and listen to the voice of conscience, when the passions are silent? This is the true philosophy, with which we must learn to be content, without envying the fame of those celebrated men, whose names are immortal in the republic of letters. Let us, instead of envying them, endeavor to make, between them and us, that honorable distinction which was formerly seen to exist between two great peoples, that the one knew how to speak, and the other how to act properly.

Here, Rousseau comes back to agree with many philosophes: virtue is something that can be known by all, "graven on every heart," and disputation over dogma is not the important point. Rather, happiness comes from one's own virtuous behavior.

EMMANUEL JOSEPH (ABBÉ) SIEYÈS

What is the Third Estate?, 1789

The Abbé Sièyes was a relative unknown when his pamphlet "What is the Third Estate?" was published in response to the French government's request for information about how the Estates General should be organized. Sieyès's argument struck a powerful chord with readers, and he was catapulted into national prominence. In this piece, Sieyès argues that the Third Estate—the commoners—are the most useful portion of the nation and therefore its only real representatives.

SOURCE: Translations and Reprints from the Original Sources of European History, *vol. VI* (Philadelphia: University of Pennsylvania, 1900), 32–35.

What is necessary that a nation should subsist and prosper? Individual effort and public functions.

All individual efforts may be included in four classes: 1. Since the earth and the waters furnish crude products for the needs of man, the first class, in logical sequence, will be that of all families which devote themselves to agricultural labor. 2. Between the first sale of products and their consumption or use, a new manipulation, more or less repeated, adds to these products a second value more or less composite. In this manner human industry succeeds in perfecting the gifts of nature, and the crude product increases two-fold, ten-fold, one hundred-fold in value. Such are the efforts of the second class.[1] 3. Between production and consumption, as well as between the various stages of production, a group of intermediary agents establish themselves, useful both to producers and consumers; these are the merchants and brokers: the brokers who, comparing incessantly the demands of time and place, speculate upon the profit of retention and transportation; merchants who are charged with distribution, in the last analysis, either at wholesale or at retail. This species of utility characterizes the third class. 4. Outside of these three classes of productive and useful citizens, who are occupied with real objects of consumption and use, there is also need in a society of a series of efforts and pains, whose objects are directly useful or agreeable to the individual. This fourth class embraces all those who stand between the most distinguished and liberal professions and the less esteemed services of domestics.

---

1. Here, by valorizing agricultural workers, merchants, and industrialists, Sieyès is turning traditional hierarchy on its head. Instead of respecting the idle rich, those who live a life of ease and luxury, Sieyès says that only those who are *useful,* who work and support society, are worthwhile.

Such are the efforts which sustain society. Who puts them forth? The Third Estate.

Public functions may be classified equally well, in the present state of affairs, under four recognized heads; the sword, the robe, the church, and the administration. It would be superfluous to take them up one by one, for the purpose of showing that everywhere the Third Estate attends to nineteen-twentieths of them, with this distinction; that it is laden with all that which is really painful, with all the burdens which the privileged classes refuse to carry.[2] Do we give the Third Estate credit for this? That this might come about, it would be necessary that the Third Estate should refuse to fill these places, or that it should be less ready to exercise their functions. The facts are well known. Meanwhile they have dared to impose a prohibition upon the order of the Third Estate. They have said to it: "Whatever may be your services, whatever may be your abilities, you shall go thus far; you may not pass beyond!" Certain rare exceptions, properly regarded, are but a mockery, and the terms which are indulged in on such occasions, one insult the more.

If this exclusion is a social crime against the Third Estate; if it is a veritable act of hostility, could it perhaps be said that it is useful to the public weal? Alas! who is ignorant of the effects of monopoly? If it discourages those whom it rejects, is it not well known that it tends to render less able those whom it favors? Is it not understood that every employment from which free competition is removed, becomes dearer and less effective?

In setting aside any function whatsoever to serve as an appanage for a distinct class among citizens, is it not to be observed that it is no longer the man alone who does the work that it is necessary to reward, but all the unemployed members of that same caste, and also the entire families of those who are employed as well as those who are not? Is it not to be remarked that since the government has become the patrimony of a particular class, it has been distended beyond all measure; places have been created, not on account of the necessities of the governed, but in the interests of the governing, etc., etc.? Has not attention been called to the fact that this order of things, which is basely and—I even presume to say—beastly respectable with us, when we find it in reading the *History of Ancient Egypt* or the accounts of *Voyages to the Indies*,[3] is despicable, monstrous, destructive of all industry, the enemy of social progress; above all degrading to the human race in general, and particularly intolerable to Europeans, etc., etc.? But I must leave these considerations, which, if they increase the importance of the subject and throw light upon it, perhaps, along with the new light, slacken our progress.

---

2. Sieyès goes further. He also denounces the system of honors and privileges within the First and Second Estates, explaining how it goes beyond damaging individuals. Rather, it results in the destruction of entire societies and limits advancement and progress.

3. Referring to the account of Indian castes in Raynal: *Histoire phil. et pol. des deux Indes*, book I., a work much in vogue at the time.

It suffices here to have made it clear that the pretended utility of a privileged order for the public service is nothing more than a chimera; that with it all that which is burdensome in this service is performed by the Third Estate; that without it the superior places would be infinitely better filled; that they naturally ought to be the lot and the recompense of ability and recognized services, and that if privileged persons have come to usurp all the lucrative and honorable posts, it is a hateful injustice to the rank and file of citizens and at the same time a treason to the public weal.

Who then shall dare to say that the Third Estate has not within itself all that is necessary for the formation of a complete nation? It is the strong and robust man who has one arm still shackled. If the privileged order should be abolished, the nation would be nothing less, but something more. Therefore, what is the Third Estate? Everything; but an everything shackled and oppressed. What would it be without the privileged order? Everything, but an everything free and flourishing. Nothing can succeed without it, everything would be infinitely better without the others.

The argument results not in a request for more opportunity— for the ability of the Third Estate to obtain honors and titles—but in a demand for the destruction of special privileges altogether.

It is not sufficient to show that privileged persons, far from being useful to the nation, cannot but enfeeble and injure it; it is necessary to prove further that the noble order does not enter at all into the social organization; that it may indeed be a burden upon the nation, but that it cannot of itself constitute a nation.

In the first place, it is not possible in the number of all the elementary parts of a nation to find a place for the *caste* of nobles. I know that there are individuals in great number whom infirmities, incapacity, incurable laziness, or the weight of bad habits render strangers to the labors of society. The exception and the abuse are everywhere found beside the rule. But it will be admitted that the less there are of these abuses, the better it will be for the State. The worst possible arrangement of all would be where not alone isolated individuals, but a whole class of citizens should take pride in remaining motionless in the midst of the general movement, and should consume the best part of the product without bearing any part in its production. Such a class is surely estranged to the nation by its indolence.

The noble order is not less estranged from the generality of us by its civil and political prerogatives.

What is a nation? A body of associates, living under a common law, and represented by the same legislature, etc.

Is it not evident that the noble order has privileges and expenditures which it dares to call its rights, but which are apart from the rights of the great body of citizens? It departs there from the common order, from the common law. So its civil rights make of it an isolated people in the midst of the great nation. This is truly *imperium in imperio.*[4]

In regard to its political rights, these also it exercises apart. It has its special representatives, which are not charged with securing the interests of the people.

---

4. *Imperium in imperio:* a state within a state, or a power within a power.

The body of its deputies sit apart; and when it is assembled in the same hall with the deputies of simple citizens, it is none the less true that its representation is essentially distinct and separate: it is a stranger to the nation, in the first place, by its origin, since its commission is not derived from the people; then by its object, which consists of defending not the general, but the particular interest.

The Third Estate embraces then all that which belongs to the nation; and all that which is not the Third Estate, cannot be regarded as being of the nation. What is the Third Estate? It is the whole.

ARTHUR YOUNG

Early Revolution in Paris, June 8, 1789

Arthur Young visited Paris shortly after the opening of the Estates General. Though he is English—and therefore possesses the liberties that Montesquieu praises in The Spirit of the Laws—*Young's tone is not entirely positive about the changes taking place in France. He provides a portrait of the mass of public opinion, as well as character outlines of an unconcerned king and some of the prominent deputies, such as the Abbé Sieyès.*

SOURCE: *James Harvey Robinson,* Readings in European History, *abr. ed. (Boston: Ginn & Co., 1906), 432–433.*

*T*he king, court, nobility, clergy, army, and parliament [i.e. *parlements*] are nearly in the same situation. All these consider with equal dread the ideas of liberty now afloat, except the first, who, for reasons obvious to those who know his character, troubles himself little, even with circumstances that concern his power the most intimately. . . .

The business going forward at present in the pamphlet shops of Paris is incredible. I went to the Palais Royal[1] to see what new things were published, and to procure a catalogue of all. Every hour produces something new. Thirteen came out to-day, sixteen yesterday, and ninety-two last week.

---

1. The Palais-Royal was land in the center of Paris owned by the Duke of Orléans, the cousin of Louis. As royal property, it was not subject to censorship. The Duke of Orléans, also called Philippe Egalité, or Philip Equality, because of his revolutionary views, encouraged wide-ranging discussions in the coffeehouses and other public places within the Palais-Royal, which led to rumors that he was trying to usurp the king. Young seems shocked by the tone of the discussion, and the listeners he's observing are at least surprised, for they listen with mouths wide open (*à gorge déployé*).

Nineteen twentieths of these productions are in favor of liberty, and commonly violent against the clergy and the nobility. I have to-day bespoke many of this description that have reputation; but inquiring for such as had appeared on the other side of the question, to my astonishment I find there are but two or three that have merit enough to be known.

But the coffee-houses in the Palais Royal present yet more singular and astonishing spectacles: they are not only crowded within, but other expectant crowds are at the doors and windows, listening *à gorge déployé* to certain orators, who from chairs or tables harangue each his little audience. The eagerness with which they are heard, and the thunder of applause they receive for every sentiment of more than common hardiness or violence against the present government, cannot easily be imagined. I am all amazement at the ministry permitting such nests and hotbeds of sedition[2] and revolt, which disseminate amongst the people every hour principles that by and by must be opposed with vigor; and therefore it seems little short of madness to allow the propagation at present.

Everything conspires to render the present period in France critical. The want of bread is terrible; accounts arrive every moment from the provinces of riots and disturbances, and calling in the military to preserve the peace of the markets. . . .

June 15. This has been a rich day, and such a one as ten years ago none could believe would ever arrive in France; a very important debate being expected on what, in our House of Commons, would be termed the state of the nation. My friend, Monsieur Lazowski, and myself were at Versailles at eight in the morning. We went immediately to the hall of the states to secure good seats in the gallery; we found some deputies already there, and a pretty numerous audience collected. The room is too large; none but stentorian lungs or the finest, clearest voices can be heard. However, the very size of the apartment, which admits two thousand people, gave a dignity to the scene. It was indeed an interesting one. The spectacle[3] of the representatives of twenty-five millions of people, just emerging from the evils of two hundred years of arbitrary power, and rising to the blessings of a freer constitution, assembled with open doors under the eye of the public, was framed to call into animated feelings every latent spark, every emotion of a liberal bosom; to banish whatever ideas might intrude of their being a people too often hostile to my own country, and to dwell with pleasure on the glorious idea of happiness to a great nation. . . .

Monsieur l'Abbé Sieyès opened the debate. He is one of the most zealous sticklers for the popular cause,—being in fact a violent republican. . . .

---

2. Young was not entirely opposed to reform, but his tone—referring to this talk as "sedition" and "madness"—makes it clear how radical this is in the context of the larger eighteenth century, even from the perspective of a man living under a constitutional monarchy.

3. Note Young's descriptions of the scene taking place and his sketches of Sieyès, Mirabeau, and Bailly. While Young is incredulous that the process he's watching could result in appropriate legislative decisions, he does find much to admire as well.

Monsieur de Mirabeau spoke without notes for near an hour, with a warmth, animation, and eloquence that entitle him to the reputation of an undoubted orator. He opposed the words "known" and "verified," in the proposition of Abbé Sieyès, with great force of reasoning, and proposed in lieu that they should declare themselves simply *Représentatives du peuple François*; that no *veto* should exist against their resolves in any other assembly; that all [existing] taxes are illegal, but should be granted during the present sessions of the states, and no longer; that the debt of the king should become the debt of the nation, and be secured on funds accordingly. Monsieur de Mirabeau was well heard, and his proposition much applauded.

In regard to their general method of proceeding, there are two circumstances in which they are very deficient. The spectators in the galleries are allowed to interfere in the debates by clapping their hands, and other noisy expressions of approbation: this is grossly indecent; it is also dangerous; for, if they are permitted to express approbation, they are, by parity of reason, allowed expressions of dissent, and they may hiss as well as clap; which it is said they have sometimes done: this would be to overrule the debate and influence the deliberations.

Another circumstance is the want of order among themselves. More than once to-day there were an hundred members on their legs at a time, and Monsieur Bailly absolutely without power to keep order.

DEPUTIES OF THE THIRD ESTATE

Decree Creating the National Assembly, June 17, 1789

Between May and June of 1789, a political stalemate existed between the Third Estate and the other two Estates, as a large number of deputies from the nobility and clergy refused to consider the idea of voting in common, while deputies from the Third Estate refused to verify their credentials separately. The impasse lasted more than a month, a period during which the deputies of the Third Estate continued to enunciate why their members were truly representative of the nation and the General Will. On June 17, these deputies proclaimed that they were the National Assembly, representative of all. Though they invited any other members who wished to join them, they refused to acknowledge any other body's political authority apart from their own.

SOURCE: *Frank Maloy Anderson*, The Constitutions and Other Select Documents, Illustrative of the History of France, 1789–1901 *(Minneapolis: Wilson Co., 1904), 1–2.*

*T*he Assembly, deliberating after the verification of the powers, recognizes that this assembly is already composed of the representatives sent directly by at least ninety-six per cent of the nation.

Such a body of deputies cannot remain inactive owing to the absence of the deputies of some bailliages and some classes of citizens; for the absentees, who have been summoned, cannot prevent those present from exercising the full extent of their rights, especially when the exercise of these rights is an imperious and pressing duty.

Furthermore, since it belongs only to the verified representatives to participate in the formation of the national opinion, and since all the verified representatives ought to be in this assembly, it is still more indispensable to conclude that the interpretation and presentation of the general will of the nation belong to it, and belong to it alone, and that there cannot exist between the throne and this assembly any *veto*, any negative power.—The Assembly declares then that the common task of the national restoration can and ought to be commenced without delay by the deputies present and that they ought to pursue it without interruption as well as without hindrance.—The denomination of NATIONAL ASSEMBLY is the only one which is suitable for the Assembly in the present condition of things; because the members who compose it are the only representatives lawfully and publicly known and verified; because they are sent directly by almost the totality of the nation; because, lastly, the representation being one and indivisible, none of the deputies, in whatever class or order he may be chosen, has the right to exercise his functions apart from the present assembly.—The Assembly will never lose the hope of uniting within its own body all the deputies absent today; it will not cease to summon them to fulfil the obligation laid upon them to participate in the holding of the States-General. At any moment when the absent deputies present themselves in the course of the session which is about to open, it declares in advance that it will hasten to receive them and to share with them, after the verification of their powers, the results of the great labors which are bound to procure the regeneration of France.—The National Assembly orders that the motives of the present decision be immediately drawn up in order to be presented to the King and the nation.

Note the early political use of Rousseau's language and questions about a veto.

DEPUTIES OF THE THIRD ESTATE

The Tennis Court Oath, June 20, 1789

On June 20, the deputies of the Third Estate, representing the commoners or, as Sieyès had claimed, the "everything" of the nation, found themselves locked out of their traditional meeting hall. Given the fact that there had been substantial agitation over questions of representation, and that the Third Estate had become increasingly politically active and vociferous in defense of their agenda, the locked door seemed a precursor to a demand that they cease their activism—a clear attempt to keep the deputies from organizing. They refused to be deterred, however, and instead gathered at an empty tennis court. At this assembly, the deputies echoed Sieyès, saying that they were the true representatives of the French nation. They pledged not to be disbanded until they had drafted a constitution for the country.

SOURCE: *Frank Maloy Anderson,* The Constitutions and Other Select Documents, Illustrative of the History of France, 1789–1901 *(Minneapolis: Wilson Co., 1904), 3.*

The National Assembly, considering that it has been summoned to determine the Constitution of the kingdom, to effect the regeneration of public order, to maintain the true principles of the monarchy; that nothing can prevent it from continuing its deliberations in whatever place it may be forced to establish itself, and lastly, that wherever its members meet together, there is the National Assembly,

Decrees that all the members of this Assembly shall immediately take a solemn oath never to separate, and to reassemble wherever circumstances shall require, until the Constitution of the kingdom shall be established and consolidated upon firm foundations; and that, the said oath being taken, all the members and each of them individually shall ratify by their signatures this stedfast resolution.

KING LOUIS XVI

Declaration of the King upon the Estates General, June 23, 1789

If Arthur Young thought Sieyès was radical, it is hardly surprising that a divine right monarch such as Louis XVI would find the rhetoric of revolutionaries, including the claim of a "National Assembly" and a demand for a constitution, entirely untenable. The king addressed all the deputies together on June 23 and attempted to end the idea that the Third Estate could possibly represent the entire nation. Louis rejected the claim of the Third Estate that it constituted a "National Assembly" and reiterated that each deputy represented only the order that had elected him. The king indicated that he was willing to compromise, however, and noted that for matters concerning all three orders, especially the pressing issue of royal fiscal policy, all the deputies could debate in common. This seemed to imply a tacit acceptance of some of the Third Estate's arguments.

SOURCE: *Frank Maloy Anderson,* The Constitutions and Other Select Documents, Illustrative of the History of France, 1789–1901 *(Minneapolis: Wilson Co., 1904), 3–5.*

1. The King wishes that the ancient distinction of the three Orders of the State be preserved in its entirety, as essentially linked to the constitution of his Kingdom; that the deputies, freely elected by each of the three Orders, forming three chambers, deliberating by Order, and being able, with the approval of the Sovereign, to agree to deliberate in common, can alone be considered as forming the body of the representatives of the Nation. As a result, the King has declared null the resolutions passed by the deputies of the Order of the Third Estate, the 17th of this month, as well as those which have followed them, as illegal and unconstitutional.

2. His Majesty declares valid all the credentials verified or to be verified in each chamber, upon which there has not been raised nor will be raised any contest; His Majesty orders that these shall be communicated by each Order respectively to the other two Orders.

As for the credentials which might be contested in each Order, and upon which the parties interested would appeal, it will be enacted, for the present session only of the States-General, as will be hereafter ordered.

* * *

7. His Majesty having exhorted the three Orders, for the safety of the State, to unite themselves during this session of Estates only, to deliberate in common upon the affairs of general utility, wishes to make his intentions known upon the manner of procedure.

8. There will be particularly excepted from the affairs which can be treated in common, (1) those that concern the ancient and constitutional rights of the three Orders, (2) the form of constitution to give the next States-General, (3) the feudal and seignorial rights, (4) the useful rights and honorary prerogatives of the two first Orders.

The especial consent of the Clergy will be necessary for all provisions which could interest religion, ecclesiastical discipline, the régime of the Orders and secular and regular bodies.

Louis XVI claims both decorum and freedom of voting require that no outsiders influence legislative deliberations. Young's critiques of the French process seem to agree and indicate that the cacophony of voices was a serious political aberration.

* * *

11. If, with the view of facilitating the reunion of the three Orders, they desired that the propositions that shall have been considered in common, should pass only by a majority of two-thirds of the votes, His Majesty is disposed to authorise this form.

* * *

15. Good order, decency, and liberty of the ballot even, require that His Majesty prohibit, as he expressly does, that any person, other than the members of the three orders comprising the States-General, should be present at their deliberations, whether they deliberate in common or separately.

NATIONAL ASSEMBLY

August Decrees, August 4–11, 1789

The fall of the Bastille and the circulation of revolutionary radicalism led to upheaval in the provinces. Some uprisings attempted to destroy those feudal arrangements which had affected the peasantry most harshly, sacking the homes of feudal lords and destroying records of obligations, including past due taxes or debts. However, as the violence grew, rumor and confusion spread fear, violence, and misery across France. The wealthy worried that they could be the next target while the poor feared the "groups of brigands" that they heard were roaming the countryside, looking for any target. A report on the condition of the provinces was read in the National Assembly on the night of August 4. While some wanted to use the report as an occasion to forcibly restore order, more deputies believed that the violence was itself a sign of problems caused by injustice stemming from privilege. Numerous deputies took to the floor to renounce feudal rights and privileges either for themselves or on behalf of the Church, cities, and provinces. Over the next week, the National Assembly finalized the form of the edict. As you read it, think about what these changes indicate about the Ancien Régime and how deputies envision the new order.

SOURCE: *Frank Maloy Anderson,* The Constitutions and Other Select Documents, Illustrative of the History of France, 1789–1901 *(Minneapolis: Wilson Co., 1904), 11–15.*

1. The National Assembly hereby completely abolishes the feudal system. It decrees that, among the existing rights and dues all those originating in or representing real or personal serfdom or personal servitude, shall be abolished without indemnification. All other dues are declared redeemable, the terms and mode of redemption to be fixed by the National Assembly. Those of the said dues which are not extinguished by this decree shall continue to be collected until indemnification shall take place.

2. The exclusive right to maintain pigeon-houses and dove-cotes is abolished. The pigeons shall be confined during the seasons fixed by the community. During

such periods they shall be looked upon as game, and every one shall have the right to kill them upon his own land.

3. The exclusive right to hunt and to maintain unenclosed warrens is likewise abolished, and every land owner shall have the right to kill or to have destroyed on his own land all kinds of game, observing, however, such police regulations as may be established with a view to the safety of the public.

All hunting captainries, including the royal forests, and all hunting rights under whatever denomination, are likewise abolished. Provision shall be made, however, in a manner compatible with the regard due to property and liberty, for maintaining the personal pleasures of the King.

The president of the assembly shall be commissioned to ask of the King the recall of those sent to the galleys or exiled, simply for violations of the hunting regulations, as well as for the release of those at present imprisoned for offences of this kind, and the dismissal of such cases as are now pending.

4. All manorial courts are hereby suppressed without indemnification. But the magistrates of these courts shall continue to perform their functions until such time as the National Assembly shall provide for the establishment of a new judicial system.

5. Tithes[1] of every description, as well as the dues which have been substituted for them, . . . as well as those devoted to the maintenance of churches, . . . are abolished, on condition, however, that some other method be devised to provide for the expenses of divine worship, the support of the officiating clergy, for the assistance of the poor, for repairs and rebuilding of churches and parsonages, and for the maintenance of all institutions, seminaries, schools, academies, asylums, and organizations to which the present funds are devoted. Until such provision shall be made and the former possessors shall enter upon the enjoyment of an income on the new system, the National Assembly decrees that the said tithes shall continue to be collected according to law and in the customary manner.

Other tithes, of whatever nature they may be, shall be redeemable in such manner as the Assembly shall determine. Until such regulation shall be issued, the National Assembly decrees that these, too, shall continue to be collected.

* * *

7. The sale of judicial and municipal offices shall be suppressed forthwith. Justice shall be dispensed *gratis*. Nevertheless, the magistrates at present holding such offices shall continue to exercise their functions and to receive their emoluments until the Assembly shall have made provision for indemnifying them.

8. The fees of the country priests are abolished, and shall be discontinued so soon as provision shall be made for increasing the minimum salary [*portion*

---

1. The tithe was a tax imposed by Church officials.

congrue] of the parish priests and the payment to the curates. A regulation shall be drawn up to determine the status of the priests in the towns.

9. Pecuniary privileges, personal or real, in the payment of taxes are abolished forever. Taxes shall be collected from all the citizens, and from all property, in the same manner and in the same form. Plans shall be considered by which the taxes shall be paid proportionally by all, even for the last six months of the current year.

10. Inasmuch as a national constitution and public liberty are of more advantage to the provinces than the privileges which some of these enjoy, and inasmuch as the surrender of such privileges is essential to the intimate union of all parts of the realm [*empire*], it is decreed that all the peculiar privileges, pecuniary or otherwise, of the provinces, principalities, districts [*pays*], cantons, cities, and communes, are once for all abolished and are absorbed into the law common to all Frenchmen.

11. All citizens, without distinction of birth, are eligible to any office or dignity, whether ecclesiastical, civil, or military; and no profession shall imply any derogation.

12. Hereafter no remittances shall be made for annates or for any other purpose to the court of Rome, the vice-legation at Avignon, or to the nunciature at Lucerne. The clergy of the diocese shall apply to their bishops in regard to the filling of benefices and dispensations, the which shall be granted *gratis* without regard to reservations, expectancies, and papal months, all the churches of France enjoying the same freedom.

13. The rights . . . established in favor of [those who] formerly exercised priestly functions . . . are abolished, but appropriate provision shall be made for those benefices of archdeacons and archpresbyters which are not sufficiently endowed.

14. Pluralities shall not be permitted hereafter in cases where the revenue from the benefice or benefices held shall exceed the sum of three thousand *livres*. Nor shall any individual be allowed to enjoy several pensions from benefices, or a pension and a benefice, if the revenue which he already enjoys from such sources exceeds the same sum of three thousand *livres*.

15. The National Assembly shall consider, in conjunction with the King, the report which is to be submitted to it relating to pensions, favors, and salaries, with a view to suppressing all such as are not deserved and reducing those which shall prove excessive; and the amount shall be fixed which the King may in the future disburse for this purpose.

16. The National Assembly decrees that a medal shall be struck in memory of the recent grave and important deliberations for the welfare of France, and that a *Te Deum* shall be chanted in gratitude in all the parishes and the churches of France.

17. The National Assembly solemnly proclaims the King, Louis XVI, the *Restorer of French Liberty*.

18. The National Assembly shall present itself in a body before the King, in order to submit to him the decrees which have just been passed, to tender to him the tokens of its most respectful gratitude and to pray him to permit the *Te Deum* to be chanted in his chapel, and to be present himself at this service.

19. The National Assembly shall consider, immediately after the constitution, the drawing up of the laws necessary for the development of the principles which it has laid down in the present decree. The latter shall be transmitted without delay by the deputies to all the provinces, together with the decree of the tenth of this month, in order that it may be printed, published, announced from the parish pulpits, and posted up wherever it shall be deemed necessary.

NATIONAL ASSEMBLY

Declaration of the Rights of Man and of the Citizen, August 26, 1789

Many of the grievances that had been submitted to the king had included a demand for a declaration of rights, a written set of guarantees that citizens could read and to which they could appeal. Like the previous document, each provision tells you about past abuses as much as future hopes. Additionally, although the idea of a declaration of rights followed an American precedent in terms of both state constitutions and national formulations, you will notice important differences between American and French understandings of civic behavior and responsibility.

SOURCE: *James Harvey Robinson,* Readings in European History, *abr. ed. (Boston: Ginn & Co., 1906), 439–441.*

The representatives of the French people, organized as a National Assembly, believing that the ignorance, neglect, or contempt of the rights of man are the sole cause of public calamities and of the corruption of governments, have determined to set forth in a solemn declaration the natural, inalienable, and sacred rights of man, in order that this declaration, being constantly before all the members of the social body, shall remind them continually of their rights and duties; in order that the acts of the legislative power, as well as those of the executive power, may be compared at any moment with the objects and purposes of all political institutions and may thus be more respected; and, lastly, in order that the grievances of the citizens, based hereafter upon simple and incontestable principles, shall tend to the maintenance of the constitution and redound to the happiness of all. Therefore the National Assembly recognizes and proclaims, in the presence and under the auspices of the Supreme Being, the following rights of man and of the citizen:

Article 1. Men are born and remain free and equal in rights.[1] Social distinctions may be founded only upon the general good.

2. The aim of all political association is the preservation of the natural and imprescriptible rights of man.[2] These rights are liberty, property, security, and resistance to oppression.

3. The principle of all sovereignty resides essentially in the nation.[3] No body nor individual may exercise any authority which does not proceed directly from the nation.

4. Liberty consists in the freedom to do everything which injures no one else; hence the exercise of the natural rights of each man has no limits except those which assure to the other members of the society the enjoyment of the same rights. These limits can only be determined by law.

5. Law can only prohibit such actions as are hurtful to society. Nothing may be prevented which is not forbidden by law, and no one may be forced to do anything not provided for by law.

6. Law is the expression of the general will.[4] Every citizen has a right to participate personally, or through his representative, in its formation. It must be the same for all, whether it protects or punishes. All citizens, being equal in the eyes of the

---

1. Men are "born free and equal in rights," with social distinctions based "only upon the general good." This marks a sharp rupture with the Ancien Régime's notion of society as an aggregation of separate orders (estates, guilds, municipalities, corporations, etc.) each possessing special duties, rights, and privileges. It is much closer to the radical social vision espoused by Sieyès.

2. Political associations exist to promote the rights of man, especially "liberty, property, security, and resistance to oppression." This entitles people to come and go as they choose and to own the property they possess. The right to property will be complicated and raises several questions. Does this include property, such as the estates of the nobility or Church entities, which may be regarded as institutionalized oppression? Does the right to resist oppression entitle someone to attack a tax collector? Can property itself become a form of oppression?

3. Sovereignty resides in the nation, which confers political rights. The nation may choose to confer special rights upon a monarch (as in the current draft of the constitution.) It cannot be the other way around.

4. "Law is the expression of the General Will." This article is the most obvious manifestation of Rousseau's centrality to the declaration. It helps identify the nation with law (i.e., a constitution) and further declares that the nation emerges from the "General Will" of the citizens. The use of the term "General Will," echoing Rousseau's term, implies the disinterested, virtuous action of the people. In Rousseau's view, the selfish will of a majority of citizens is what he calls "the will of all." That is not the same as the General Will, which emerges only when citizens act disinterestedly, heeding only the needs of the polity. The implication here is that a citizen is a citizen only when being virtuous. The General Will is the collective will of the virtuous citizenry.

law, are equally eligible to all dignities and to all public positions and occupations, according to their abilities, and without distinction except that of their virtues and talents.

7. No person shall be accused, arrested, or imprisoned except in the cases and according to the forms prescribed by law.[5] Any one soliciting, transmitting, executing, or causing to be executed, any arbitrary order, shall be punished. But any citizen summoned or arrested in virtue of the law shall submit without delay, as resistance constitutes an offense.

8. The law shall provide for such punishments only as are strictly and obviously necessary, and no one shall suffer punishment except it be legally inflicted in virtue of a law passed and promulgated before the commission of the offense.

9. As all persons are held innocent until they shall have been declared guilty, if arrest shall be deemed indispensable, all harshness not essential to the securing of the prisoner's person shall be severely repressed by law.

10. No one shall be disquieted on account of his opinions, including his religious views, provided their manifestation does not disturb the public order established by law.[6]

11. The free communication of ideas and opinions is one of the most precious of the rights of man. Every citizen may, accordingly, speak, write, and print with freedom, but shall be responsible for such abuses of this freedom as shall be defined by law.

12. The security of the rights of man and of the citizen requires public military forces. These forces are, therefore, established for the good of all and not for the personal advantage of those to whom they shall be intrusted.

13. A common contribution is essential for the maintenance of the public forces and for the cost of administration. This should be equitably distributed among all the citizens in proportion to their means.[7]

14. All the citizens have a right to decide, either personally or by their representatives, as to the necessity of the public contribution; to grant this freely; to know to what uses it is put; and to fix the proportion, the mode of assessment, and of collection and the duration of the taxes.

---

5. Those members of a nation who resist or oppose its law (i.e., the virtuous "General Will" of the nation) are guilty of a political crime that warrants punishment.

6. Freedom of worship and speech is a right of all citizens, "provided their manifestation does not disturb the public order established by law." These articles are directed in part at the Catholic Church, which had campaigned, sometimes successfully, to outlaw Protestant worship. Some of those in England who embraced the French Revolution did so because it weakened the power of the Church. This guarantee will be a two-edged sword, however. What does public order and freedom of worship mean in the context of civil war?

7. Taxes are to be apportioned "equally" and "according to the means" of citizens. No longer will privileged orders receive preferential tax treatment (as with the clergy, nobility, and special corporations.)

15. Society has the right to require of every public agent an account of his administration.[8]

16. A society in which the observance of the law is not assured, nor the separation of powers defined, has no constitution at all.[9]

17. Since property is an inviolable and sacred right,[10] no one shall be deprived thereof except where public necessity, legally determined, shall clearly demand it, and then only on condition that the owner shall have been previously and equitably indemnified.

---

8. People have the right to demand an accounting of public officials, and even to charge them with crimes. Officials serve the people; it cannot be the other way around.

9. "Any society in which the observance of the law is not assured, nor the separation of powers defined, has no constitution at all." This does not clearly state how the separation of powers is determined, but when read in conjunction with the articles locating sovereignty within the nation and defining the nation in terms of the General Will of the people as a whole, Article 16 suggests that the legislature is supreme and the monarch (or executive function) is merely charged with executing the laws.

10. This (again) reinforces the property clause (Article 2) by defining property as "an inviolable and sacred right."

ALEXANDRE LAMETH

Origin of the Jacobin Club, 1789

In this source, one of the most prominent early members of the Jacobin Club, Alexandre Lameth, talks about how the Club, originally called the Society of the Friends of the Constitution, was formed. He lists names of prominent members whom you will recognize in this game and explains why they decided to meet together to discuss political ideas and the events in the National Assembly before advancing to the floor with legislation.

SOURCE: *James Harvey Robinson,* Readings in European History, *abr. ed. (Boston: Ginn & Co., 1906), 451–452.*

After the transfer of the Assembly to Paris [October, 1789], the deputies from provinces which were distant from the capital, and who, for the most part, had never visited Paris (for traveling was not so easy then as it is now), experienced a sort of terror at the idea of being alone and, so to speak, lost in the midst of this huge city. They almost all, consequently, endeavored to lodge as near as possible to the Assembly, which then sat near the Feuillants (at the point where the Rue de Rivoli and the Rue Castiglione[1] now intersect), in order that they might be easily found in case of necessity.

But they were desirous that there should also be a place where they might come together in order to agree upon the attitude that they should take toward public questions. They applied, therefore, for information to residents of the capital in whom they had confidence; a search was then made in the neighborhood of the Assembly, and the refectory of the convent of the Jacobins was leased for two hundred francs a year as a place of meeting. The necessary furniture, which consisted of chairs, together with tables for the committee, was procured for a like sum.

At the first session about one hundred deputies were present, the next day double that number. The Baron de Menou was elected president, and Target, Barnave, Alexandre de Lameth, Le Chapelier, and Adrien du Port were elected secretaries, as well as three others whose names have escaped me.

A committee was chosen to draw up a list of regulations, of which Barnave was the chairman. The society decided on the name Friends of the Constitution. It was determined that all members of the Assembly should be admitted, but only such other persons should be received as had published useful works. The first to be thus received were Condorcet, the Marquis de Casotte, a distinguished economist, the Abbé Lecamus, a mathematician, and a small number of other savants or publicists.

The aim of the Society of the Friends of the Constitution was to discuss questions which were already, or were about to be placed, upon the calendar of the National Assembly. It cannot be denied that, inasmuch as the non-deputies present exercised no restraint upon these discussions, they often had more force and brilliancy than in the Assembly itself, where one found himself hindered by the violent contradictions of the right wing, and often intimidated by a crowd of spectators.[2]

This preliminary consideration shed a great deal of light upon the discussions in the Assembly. The resolve to decide within the society itself, by preliminary ballots, the nominees for president, secretaries, and the committees of the Assembly, proved a great advantage to the popular party; for from that time the elections were almost always carried by the left, although up to that time they had been almost entirely controlled by the right. Camus, an ecclesiastical lawyer, then president and since become a republican, had been elected by the aristocracy.

---

1. You can find these locations on the Map (p. 26).

2. Notice the importance of evening discussion in the Jacobin Club, before issues were brought to the Assembly floor. This preparation is part of what set Jacobins apart from the deputies on the right.

The number of the deputies who customarily frequented the Society of the Friends of the Constitution quickly rose to nearly four hundred. The number of writers also increased in a marked ratio. But it was not long before the condition of having published a useful book was no longer required for admission to the society, and it was decided that it was sufficient to have been recommended by six members. The organization then grew larger, and no longer possessed the same solidity in its composition. Very soon the place of meeting became insufficient, and permission was obtained from the monks of the convent to meet in their library, and later in their church.

Along in December, 1789, many of the leading inhabitants of the provinces, having come to Paris either on private business or to follow more closely the course of public affairs, had themselves introduced at the society and expressed a desire to establish similar ones in the chief cities of France; for they felt that these associations of citizens intent upon defending the cause of public interest would form an efficient means of counteracting the violent opposition of the aristocracy, a class which had not yet lost the power which it had so long exercised.

NATIONAL ASSEMBLY

Decrees on Church Lands and Monastic Vows, November to February, 1789

As you read these decrees, think back to Voltaire's argument about the pernicious role of religion in public life. The general attitude of the National Assembly toward religion seems to grow increasingly close to Voltaire's attitude, especially as it attempts to place the Church in a subordinate position. Think also about the abuses that the Revolution attempted to rectify and why the Church might be seen as a threat by the deputies. Why is the National Assembly interested in proceeding this way?

SOURCE: *Frank Maloy Anderson*, The Constitutions and Other Select Documents, Illustrative of the History of France, 1789–1901 *(Minneapolis: Wilson Co., 1904), 15–16.*

The National Assembly decrees, 1st, All the ecclesiastical estates are at the disposal of the nation, on condition of providing in a suitable manner for the expenses of worship, the maintenance of its ministers, and the relief of the poor, under the supervision and following the directions of the provinces; 2d, that in the provisions to be made, in order to provide for the maintenance of the ministers of religion, there can be assured for the endowment of each curé *not less than twelve hundred livres per annum*, not including the dwelling and the gardens attached.

B. DECREE UPON MONASTIC VOWS. FEBRUARY 13, 1789

1. The constitutional law of the kingdom shall no longer recognize solemn monastic vows of persons of either sex; in consequence, the orders and congregations living according to rule are and shall remain suppressed in France, without there being any similar ones allowed in the future.

2. All the persons of either sex living in the monasteries and religious houses may leave them by making their declaration before the municipality of the place, and there shall immediately be provision made for their existence by a suitable pension. There shall also be houses set aside to which the religious who do not wish to profit by the provision of the present [article] shall be required to retire. Moreover, there shall be no change for the present in respect to the houses charged with public education and the establishments of charity and any that have until now taken part in these matters.

3. The religious shall be able to remain in the houses in which they are at present, excepting those described in the article which requires the religious to unite several houses into one.

NATIONAL ASSEMBLY

Decree Regarding Membership in the National Guard, June 12, 1790

In response to the rise of multiple local military groups across France, the National Assembly ordered that all such groups would be subsumed within the National Guard, and that the National Guard would be made up only of active citizens. In this decree, the National Assembly restricted membership in the National Guard to "active citizens" and their sons. An active citizen was understood to be a male who paid taxes equivalent to three days' wages. "Passive citizens"—women, domestic servants, and all those with insufficient property to pay such a tax—were purposely excluded from the National Guard. This means that about one-half of the male population of France at the time was excluded from participation.

SOURCE: *M. J. Mavidal and M.E. Laurent, dirs.* Archives parlementaires de 1787 à 1860: Recueil complet des débats législatifs et politiques des chambres françaises, Du 31 mai au 8 juillet 1790, vol. 16, trans. *Jennifer Popiel (Paris: Librairie administrative de Paul Dupont, 1883) 184–85.*

*M*r. Target proposed, in the name of the Constitutional Committee, to order that all military bodies that currently exist in the town of Caen be incorporated into the national militia in order to continue in service. Further, they would be required to wear uniforms and the national cockade, according to the terms of the king's proclamation.

It was then requested that this decree be made generally applicable for every location where there are National Guards.

As a result, two decrees were adopted in the following terms. . . .

The National Assembly, following the report of its Constitutional Committee . . . decrees that said ordinance and said regulation will be provisionally carried out until the final organization of the National Guards, on the following conditions:

1. In the month following the publication of this decree, all active citizens who wish to continue to exercise the rights attached in this manner will be required to inscribe their names in the section of the city where they live, in a register that will be opened for the purpose of service in the National Guard.

2. The children of active citizens who are themselves at least 18 years old may equally be inscribed in the same register. If they are not, they may not bear arms nor be employed even as replacements for those already in service.

3. Active citizens whose circumstances, age and infirmities, or other impediments render them unfit to serve personally should be replaced. They may not be replaced except by active citizens or by their children, as inscribed in these registers of the National Guard.

* * *

5. No citizen may bear arms if he is not registered in the manner which has been determined. Accordingly, all special bodies of citizen militias, musketeers, or any other of whatever description will be required to be incorporated into the National Guard, in the uniform of the nation, under the same flag, the same order, the same officers and staff. Any different uniform, any cockade other than the national cockade, must be reformed according to the terms of the king's proclamation. The flags of the old regiments and companies will be hung from the roof of the principal church of the town, and will remain there, dedicated to union, harmony, and peace.

Note how the Church is expected to fulfil a civic and military function in the last sentence of this document. What does that say about its role in the Revolutionary regime?

NATIONAL ASSEMBLY

Decree Abolishing the Nobility, June 19, 1790

The demand for social equality, borne out of frustration with privilege and hierarchical organization, came to a logical conclusion in June 1790. On June 19, the National Assembly went beyond abolishing feudal privilege and attempted to remake social status, too.

SOURCE: *Frank Maloy Anderson,* The Constitutions and Other Select Documents, Illustrative of the History of France, 1789–1901 *(Minneapolis: Wilson Co., 1904), 34.*

1. Hereditary nobility is forever abolished; in consequence the titles of prince, duke, count, marquis, viscount, vidame, baron, knight, *messire, ecuyer noble,* and all other similar titles, shall neither be taken by anyone whomsoever nor given to anybody.

2. A citizen may take only the true name of his family; no one may wear liveries nor cause them to be worn, nor have armorial bearings; incense shall not be burned in the temples, except in order to honor the Divinity, and shall not be offered for any one whomsoever.

3. The titles of *monseigneur* and *messeigneurs* shall not be given to any body [of men] nor to any person, likewise the titles of excellency, highness, eminence, grace, etc.

NATIONAL ASSEMBLY

Civil Constitution of the Clergy, July 12, 1790

This law made the Church subordinate to the French State. While land had already been confiscated and monastic vows banned, the Civil Constitution regularized dioceses so that they would match all new administrative districts. It also prevented high church officials from taking vows to any foreign power (namely, the pope). Bishops and priests would be elected by the people (rather than being chosen by the church hierarchy), a move which subordinated even the clergy to popular sovereignty. Perhaps most tellingly, bishops could not request confirmation from the pope but were required to publicly affirm their loyalty to the nation. Salaries were to be paid by the national government, making it even clearer that accountability was to the state, not to the Church.

SOURCE: *Frank Maloy Anderson,* The Constitutions and Other Select Documents, Illustrative of the History of France, 1789–1901 *(Minneapolis: Wilson Co., 1904), 16–22.*

The National Assembly, after having heard the report of the Ecclesiastical Committee, has decreed and does decree the following as constitutional articles:—

TITLE I

1. Each department shall form a single diocese, and each diocese shall have the same extent and the same limits as the department.

All other bishoprics in the eighty-three departments of the kingdom . . . are, and forever shall be, abolished.

The kingdom shall be divided into ten metropolitan districts, of which the sees shall be situated at Rouen, Rheims, Besançon, Rennes, Paris, Bourges, Bordeaux, Toulouse, Aix, and Lyons.

* * *

4. No church or parish of France nor any French citizen may acknowledge upon any occasion or upon any pretext whatsoever, the authority of an ordinary bishop or of an archbishop whose see shall be under the supremacy of a foreign power, nor that of their representatives residing in France or elsewhere; without prejudice, however, to the unity of the faith and the intercourse which shall be maintained with the Visible Head of the Universal Church, as hereafter provided.

5. After the bishop of a diocese shall have rendered his decision in his synod upon the matters lying within his competence an appeal may be carried to the archbishop, who shall give his decision in the metropolitan synod.

6. A new arrangement and division of all the parishes of the kingdom shall be undertaken immediately in concert with the Bishop and the District Administration. The number and extent of the parishes shall be determined according to rules which shall be laid down.

* * *

15. There shall be but a single parish in all cities and towns having not more than 6,000 inhabitants. The other parishes shall be abolished or absorbed into that of the Episcopal church.

16. In cities having a population of more than 6,000 inhabitants a parish may include a greater number of parishioners, and as many parishes shall be perpetuated as the needs of the people and localities shall require.

17. The administrative assemblies, in concert with the bishop of the diocese, shall indicate to the next legislative assembly, the country and subordinate urban parishes which ought to be contracted or enlarged, established, or abolished, and shall indicate farther the limits of the parishes as the needs of the people, the dignity of religion and the various localities shall require.

* * *

20. All titles and offices other than those mentioned in the present constitution, *dignites*, canonries, prebends, half-prebends, chapels, chaplainships, both in cathedral and collegiate churches, all regular and secular chapters for either sex, abbacies, and priorships, both regular and *in commendam*, for either sex, as well as all other benefices and prestimonies in general, of whatever kind or denomination, are from the day of this decree extinguished and abolished and shall never be re-established in any form.

* * *

TITLE II

1. Beginning with the day of publication of the present decree there shall be but one mode of choosing bishops and parish priests, namely that of election.

2. All elections shall be by ballot and shall be decided by the absolute majority of the votes.

3. The election of bishops shall take place according to the forms and by the electoral body designated in the decree of December 22, 1789, for the election of members of the Departmental Assembly.

* * *

6. The election of a bishop can only take place or be undertaken upon Sunday, in the principal church of the chief town of the department, at the close of the parish mass, at which all the electors are required to be present.

7. In order to be eligible to a bishopric one must have fulfilled for fifteen years at least the duties of the church ministry in the diocese as a parish priest, officiating minister or curate or as superior or as directing vicar of the seminary.

* * *

17. The archbishop or senior bishop of the province shall have the right to examine the bishop-elect in the presence of his council upon his belief and his character. If he deems him fit for the position he shall give him the canonical institution. If he believes it his duty to refuse this, the reasons for his refusal shall be recorded in writing and signed by the archbishop and his council, reserving to the parties concerned the right to appeal on the ground of an abuse of power as hereinafter provided.

18. The bishop applied to for institution may not exact of the person elected any form of oath except that he makes profession of the Roman Catholic and Apostolic religion.

19. The new bishop may not apply to the pope for any form of conformation, but shall write to him as the Visible Head of the Universal Church as a testimony to the unity of faith and communion maintained with him.

* * *

21. Before the ceremony of consecration begins, the bishop-elect shall take a solemn oath in the presence of the municipal officers, of the people and of the clergy to guard with care the faithful of his diocese who are confided to him, to be loyal to the Nation, the Law and the King and to support with all his power the constitution decreed by the National Assembly and accepted by the King.

* * *

25. The election of the parish priests shall take place according to the forms and by the electors designated in the decree of December 22, 1789, for the election of members of the Administrative Assembly of the District.

* * *

29. Each elector, before depositing his ballot in the ballot-box, shall take oath to vote only for that person whom he has conscientiously selected in his heart as the most worthy, without having been influenced by any gift, promise, solicitation, or threat. The same oath shall be required at the election of the bishops as in the case of the parish priests.

* * *

40. Bishoprics and *cures* shall be looked upon as vacant until those elected to fill them shall have taken the oath above mentioned.

* * *

TITLE III

1. The ministers of religion, performing as they do the first and most important functions of society and forced to live continuously in the place where they discharge the offices to which they have been called by the confidence of the people, shall be supported by the nation.

* * *

5. The salaries of the parish priests shall be as follows: In Paris, 6000 *livres*; in cities having a population of 50,000 or over, 4000 *livres*; in those having a population of less than 50,000 and more than 10,000, 3000 *livres*; in cities and towns of which the population is below 10,000 and more than 3000, 2400 *livres*.

In all other cities, towns and villages where the parish shall have a population between 3000 and 2500, 2000 *livres;* in those between 2500 and 2000, 1800 *livres;* in those having a population of less than 2000, and more than 1000, the salary shall be 1500 *livres;* in those having 1000 inhabitants and under, 1200 *livres.*

* * *

12. In view of the salary which is assured to them by the present constitution, the bishops, parish priests and curates shall perform the episcopal and priestly functions *gratis.*

TITLE IV

1. The law requiring the residence of ecclesiastics in the districts under their charge shall be strictly observed. All vested with an ecclesiastical office or function shall be subject to this without distinction or exception.

2. No bishop shall absent himself from his diocese more than two weeks consecutively during the year, except in case of real necessity and with the consent of the Directory of the Department in which his see is situated.

3. In the same manner the parish priests and the curates may not absent themselves from the place of their duties beyond the term fixed above, except for weighty reasons, and even in such cases the priests must obtain the permission both of their bishop and of the Directory of their district, and the curates that of the parish priest.

4. In case a bishop or a priest shall violate this law requiring residence, the communal government shall inform the *procureur-general syndic* of the department, who shall issue a summons to him to return to his duties. After a second warning the procureur shall take steps to have his salary declared forfeited for the whole period of his absence.

* * *

6. Bishops, parish priests, and curates may, as active citizens, be present at the Primary and Electoral Assemblies, they may be chosen electors or as deputies to the Legislative Body, or as members of the General Council of the Communes or of the Administrative Councils of their districts or departments. Their duties are, however, declared incompatible with those of *Maire* or other municipal officers and those of the members of the Directories of the District and of the Department. If elected to one of these last mentioned offices they must make a choice between it and their ecclesiastical position.

7. The incompatibility of office mentioned in article 6 shall only be observed in the future. If any bishops, parish priests, or curates have been called by their fellow-citizens to the offices of *Maire* or to other communal offices or have been elected members of the Directory of the District or of the Department they may continue their functions.

NATIONAL ASSEMBLY

Obligatory Oath, November 27, 1790

Increasingly widespread resistance to the Civil Constitution, including opposition from priests who had initially supported the document, led the National Assembly to add an additional section to the Civil Constitution, one that required all Church officials to swear an oath of fidelity to the nation or be deprived of their office.

SOURCE: *Frank Maloy Anderson,* The Constitutions and Other Select Documents, Illustrative of the History of France, 1789–1901 *(Minneapolis: Wilson Co., 1904), 22–23.*

1. The bishops and former archbishops and the cures kept in their positions shall be required, if they have not already done so, to take the oath for which they are liable, concerning the Civil Constitution of the Clergy. In consequence, they shall swear...to look with care after the faithful of their diocese or the parish which is entrusted to them, to be faithful to the nation, to the law and to the King, and to maintain with all their power the constitution decreed by the National Assembly and accepted by the King.

2. [The same requirement, except the first clause, is made of "all other ecclesiastical public functionaries."]

* * *

5. Those of the said bishops, former archbishops, cures, and other ecclesiastical public functionaries, who shall not have taken...the oath which is prescribed for them respectively, shall be reputed to have renounced their office and there shall be provision made for their replacement, as in case of vacancy by the resignation.

POPE PIUS VI

Charitas: On the Civil Oath in France, April 13, 1791

The current Pope denounced the Civil Constitution of the Clergy and rebuked King Louis XVI for signing the document. In this papal bull, he flayed the National Assembly and ordered Catholic clergy to repudiate any vows taken or performed under its auspices. He declared during clergy (i.e., those who had sworn the oath) to be in schism, or completely separated from the Catholic Church.

SOURCE: *Carlen, Claudia, ed. The papal encyclicals. Volume 1. (Wilmington, N.C.: McGrath Pub. Co., 1981), pp. 177–184.*

*T*o Our Beloved Sons, the Cardinals of the Holy Roman Church, to Our Venerable Brothers the Archbishops and Bishops, and to Our Beloved Children . . . of the Kingdom of France.

. . . We have just learned of the war against the Catholic religion which has been started by the revolutionary thinkers who as a group form a majority in the National Assembly of France. We have wept in God's presence, shared Our sorrow with the cardinals, and proclaimed public and private prayers. Then We wrote to King Louis, on July 9, 1790, and repeatedly encouraged him not to confirm the Civil Constitution of the Clergy which would lead his people into error and schism. For it was intolerable that a political assembly should change the universal practice of the Church, disregard the opinions of the holy Fathers and the decrees of the councils, overturn the order of the hierarchy and control the election of bishops, destroy episcopal sees, and introduce a worse form into the Church after removing the better.

3. We sent two briefs on the following day to the archbishops of Bordeaux and Vienne who were with the king, urging them in fatherly fashion to advise the king that if he lent his authority to this Constitution, his kingdom would be in schism; furthermore We would regard any bishops appointed in accordance with its decrees as schismatic and lacking all ecclesiastical jurisdiction. To remove all doubt that Our concern was solely with matters of religion and to silence the enemies of this Apostolic See, We gave orders that the collection of taxes from French revenues should be discontinued, although these taxes were due for Our services from unbroken custom and earlier agreements.

4. The king would certainly have refrained from approving the Constitution, but the National Assembly finally forced him to lend his authority to the Constitution as his letters to Us on July 28, September 6, and December 16 attest. He besought Us insistently to approve five, and later seven, articles at least provisionally. These articles were so similar in tenor that they formed a comprehensive summary of the new Constitution.

5. We saw at once, of course, that We could approve or tolerate none of the articles since they were at variance with canonical regulations. However, We did not want to give Our enemies an opportunity to deceive the nations by claiming that We were opposed to every sort of negotiations: therefore We told the King in Our letter of August 17 that We would consider the articles carefully and consult with the cardinals, who would meet to discuss every aspect of the proposal.

. . . We were greatly consoled when a majority of the French bishops firmly opposed the Constitution and attacked every point in it which referred to the government of the Church . . . We were further consoled because many other bishops joined the thirty in accepting this explanation. Only four out of one hundred and thirty-one bishops dissented . . . most of the parish priests and lower clergy also joined the bishops. So this explanation, accepted with harmonious unanimity, should be regarded as the teaching of the entire French Church.

. . . The decrees provided that all pastors should swear unequivocally that they would observe the Constitution already published and the one which was to be published later. Those who refused were to be considered expelled from their office, and their sees and parishes were to lose their pastor. When the lawful pastors and ministers were driven out, by force if necessary, the municipal districts could set about electing new bishops and parish priests. . . .

Almost all the bishops and most of the parish priests have refused the oath with unconquerable firmness. The enemies of religion then realized correctly that their vicious plans would come to nothing unless they persuaded some bishop, either by appealing to his ambition or his stupidity, to take the oath to observe the Constitution and to undertake sacrilegious consecrations and so, to initiate a schism.

11. . . . After examining all the articles in order to make clear to everyone that in the judgment of this Holy See, which has been sought by the French bishops and is eagerly awaited by French Catholics, We declared that the new Constitution of the Clergy is composed of principles derived from heresy. It is consequently heretical in many of its decrees and at variance with Catholic teaching. In other decrees it is sacrilegious and schismatic. It overturns the rights and primacy of the Church, is opposed to ancient and modern practice, and is devised and published with the sole design of utterly destroying the Catholic religion. For it is only this religion which cannot be freely professed, whose lawful pastors are removed, and whose property is taken over. Men of other sects are left at liberty and in possession of their property. . . .

20. From this series of sins schism is being introduced and spread in the kingdom of France, which is so dear to Us and has served religion so well; for the same reason pastors of first and second rank are being everywhere elected as the days go by, legitimate ministers are ejected from their positions, and ravening wolves are put in their place. We are certainly saddened by this sorrowful situation. Therefore to hinder the spread of schism from the start, to recall to their duty those who have strayed, to fortify the good in their purpose, and to preserve religion in that prosperous kingdom, We follow the advice of the Cardinals and answer the prayers of the entire group of bishops of the French church. Imitating the example of Our predecessors, We proclaim that each and every cardinal, archbishop, bishop, abbot, vicar, canon, parish priest, curate, and member of the clergy, whether secular or regular, who has purely and simply taken the Civil Oath as ordered by the National Assembly is suspended from the exercise of his office and will act irregularly if he exercises his office unless he abjures his oath within forty days from this date. For the oath is the poisoned source and origin of all errors and the chief cause of the sorrow of the French Catholic church.

* * *

We prohibit severely both those who have been or are to be elected as bishops from rashly accepting episcopal consecration from any metropolitan or bishop as well as the spurious bishops and their sacrilegious consecrators and all other archbishops and bishops from daring to consecrate on any pretext those who have been or are to be wrongfully elected. Furthermore, We command those who have been or are to be elected, to behave in no way as archbishops, bishops, parish priests, or vicars nor to call themselves by the name of any cathedral or parochial church, nor to assume any jurisdiction, authority, or faculty for the care of souls under the penalty of suspension and invalidity. None of those who have been named can ever be freed from the punishment of suspension, except by Us or by delegates of the Apostolic See.

27. With the greatest possible kindness, We have declared the canonical penalties imposed until the present in order that the evil deeds already accomplished may be corrected and prevented from spreading abroad. We hope in the Lord that the consecrators, the intruders in cathedral and parochial churches, and all the authors and supporters of the published Constitution will recognize their error and return repentant to the fold from which they were seduced by treacherous deceit.

. . . 32. At length We beseech you all, beloved Catholic children, in the kingdom of France; as you recall the religion and faith of your fathers, We urge you lovingly not to abandon it. For it is the one true religion which both confers eternal life and makes safe and thriving civil societies. Carefully beware of lending your ears to the treacherous speech of the philosophy of this age which leads to death. Keep away from all intruders, whether called archbishops, bishops, or parish priests; do not hold communion with them especially in divine worship. Listen carefully to the message of your lawful pastors who are still living, and who will be put in charge of you later, according to the canons. Finally, in one word, stay close to Us. For no one can be in the Church of Christ without being in unity with its visible head and founded on the See of Peter.

To inspire all to fulfill their duties more ardently, We implore the heavenly Father to send you the Spirit of counsel, truth, and constancy. As a pledge of Our paternal love, beloved sons, venerable brothers and beloved children, We impart to you the Apostolic blessing.

Given at Rome in St. Peter's under the Ring of the Fisherman on April 13, 1791, in the seventeenth year of Our pontificate.

NATIONAL ASSEMBLY

Constitution of 1791

Parts of this have been passed, though not formally added to the final constitution. (For example, the Declaration of the Rights of Man and of the Citizen *has already been passed.) It will be your task to decide what should be included in the final document and in what form.*

SOURCE: *Frank Maloy Anderson,* The Constitutions and Other Select Documents, Illustrative of the History of France, 1789–1901 *(Minneapolis: Wilson Co., 1904), 60–93.*

*T*he National Assembly, wishing to establish the French Constitution upon the principles that it has just recognized and declared, abolishes irrevocably the institutions that have injured liberty and the equality of rights.

There is no longer nobility, nor peerage, nor hereditary distinctions, nor distinction of orders, nor feudal régime, nor patrimonial jurisdictions, nor any titles, denominations or prerogatives derived therefrom, nor any order of chivalry, nor any corporations or decorations which demanded proofs of nobility or that were grounded upon distinctions of birth, nor any superiority other than that of public officials in the exercise of their functions.

There is no longer either sale or inheritance of any public office.

There is no longer for any part of the nation nor for any individual any privilege or exception to the law that is common to all Frenchmen.

The law no longer recognizes religious vows nor any other obligation which may be contrary to natural rights or the constitution.

TITLE I. FUNDAMENTAL PROVISIONS GUARANTEED BY THE CONSTITUTION[1]

The constitution guarantees as natural and civil rights:

1. That all the citizens are eligible to offices and employments without any other distinction than that of virtue and talent;

2. That all the taxes shall be equally apportioned among all the citizens in proportion to their means. . . .

---

1. Title I roots the constitution in natural law, which transcends human agency. An assumption is that natural law, like scientific law, is bound up with the functioning of the world. Because of natural law, people possess natural rights, including the liberty "to move about, to remain, and to depart without liability," and the liberty "to speak, to write, to print and publish," and so on, as in the *Declaration of the Rights of Man and of the Citizen.* Such rights, however, are subject to certain constraints. For example, citizens retain the freedom to meet "peaceably and without arms," but they are obliged to obey "the police laws." Similarly, the legislature cannot infringe on a citizen's natural rights, but it can "establish penalties against acts which . . . may be injurious to society." The constitution also reiterates the "inviolability of property." Social welfare and education now become obligations of the state, not of private charity or the Catholic Church.

The constitution likewise guarantees as natural and civil rights:

Liberty to every man to move about, to remain, and to depart without liability to arrest or detention, except according to the forms determined by the constitution;

Liberty to every man to speak, to write, to print and publish his ideas without having his writings subjected to any censorship or inspection before their publication, and to follow the religious worship to which he is attached;

Liberty to the citizens to meet peaceably and without arms, in obedience to the police laws;

Liberty to address individually signed petitions to the constituted authorities.

The legislative power cannot make any law that attacks and impedes the exercise of the natural and civil rights contained in the present title and guaranteed by the constitution; but as liberty consists only in the power to do anything that is not injurious to the rights of others or to the public security, the law can establish penalties against acts which, in attacking the public security or the rights of others, may be injurious to society.

The constitution guarantees the inviolability of property or a just and prior indemnity for that of which a legally established public necessity may demand the sacrifice.

Property intended for the expenses of worship and for all services of public utility belongs to the nation and is at all times at its disposal. . . .

The citizens have the right to elect or choose the ministers of their religious sects.[2]

There shall be created and organized a general establishment of *public relief* to bring up abandoned children, to relieve infirm paupers, and to provide work for the able-bodied poor who may not have been able to obtain it for themselves.

There shall be created and organized a *system of public instruction*, common to all citizens, gratuitous as regards the parts of education indispensable for all men, and whose establishments shall be gradually distributed in accordance with the division of the kingdom.

There shall be established national fêtes to preserve the memory of the French Revolution, to maintain fraternity among the citizens, and to attach them to the constitution, the fatherland, and the laws.

A code of civil laws common to all the kingdom shall be made.

TITLE II. OF THE DIVISION OF THE KINGDOM AND OF THE CONDITION OF THE CITIZENS

1. The kingdom is one and indivisible; its territory is divided into eighty-three departments, each department into districts, each district into cantons.

* * *

---

2. What about ministers who refuse to swear an oath of loyalty?

5. The civic oath is: *I swear to be faithful to the nation, the law, and the King, and to maintain with all my power the constitution of the kingdom decreed by the National Constituent Assembly in the years 1789, 1790, and 1791.*

* * *

7. The law considers marriage as only a civil contract.[3]

* * *

TITLE III. OF THE PUBLIC POWERS

1. Sovereignty is one, indivisible, inalienable, and imprescriptible: it belongs to the nation: no section of the people nor any individual can attribute to himself the exercise thereof.[4]

2. The nation, from which alone emanates all the powers, can exercise them only by delegation.

The French constitution is representative; the representatives are the Legislative Body and the King.

3. The legislative power is delegated to one National Assembly, composed of temporary representatives freely elected by the people, in order to be exercised by it with the sanction of the King in the manner which shall be determined hereinafter.

4. The government is monarchical: the executive power is delegated to the King, in order to be exercised under his authority by ministers and other responsible agents, in the manner which shall be determined hereinafter.

5. The judicial power is delegated to judges elected at stated times by the people.

CHAPTER I. OF THE NATIONAL LEGISLATIVE ASSEMBLY

1. The National Assembly, forming the Legislative Body, is permanent and is composed of only one chamber.[5]

---

3. Title II establishes a new, more rational division of the country into departments, outlines the text of the civic oath, and removes from the Catholic Church legal authority over marriage. That is, marriage is transformed into a civil contract, subject to laws set by the National Assembly. Couples can still choose to consecrate their relation through the rites of the Catholic Church, but that religious ceremony will have no legal significance.

4. The language here echoes Rousseau as it outlines the fundamental principle that sovereignty resides with the people of France as expressed in their legislature (the National Assembly). Listen for echoes of the *Social Contract* when you read the introduction explaining that sovereignty is "one, indivisible, inalienable, and imprescriptible: it belongs to the nation: no section of the people nor any individual can attribute to himself the exercise thereof."

5. The legislature's power itself is not to be divided. Unlike the British legislature or the American Congress, the French legislature is to be an undivided expression of the will of the French people. It will therefore consist of a unicameral (one body) legislature, re-elected every two years.

2. It shall be formed every two years by new elections. Each period of two years shall constitute a legislature.

* * *

5. The Legislative Body shall not be dissolved by the King.

* * *

Section II. Primary assemblies.—Selection of the electors

* * *

2. In order to be an active citizen it is necessary to be born or to become a Frenchman; to be fully twenty-five years of age; to be domiciled in the city or in the canton for the time fixed by the law;

To pay in some place of the kingdom a direct tax at the least equal to the value of three days of labor, and to present the receipt therefor;

Not to be in a state of domestic service, that is to say, not to be a servant for wages;

To be registered upon the roll of the national guards in the municipality of his domicile;

To have taken the civic oath.[6]

* * *

7. No one can be chosen an elector if he does not unite with the conditions necessary to be an active citizen, the following:

In the cities over six thousand souls, that of being proprietor of an estate valued upon the tax rolls at a at a revenue equal to the local value of two hundred days of labor.

* * *

And in the country, . . . that of being the farmer valued upon the same rolls at the value of four hundred days of labor.

* * *

2. The representatives and the substitutes shall be elected by majority of the votes, and they shall be chosen only from among the active citizens of the department.

---

6. The Constitution requires certain property qualifications to be an active citizen, and more stringent qualifications to be an elector. According to this system, active citizens gather in their local towns to elect "electors," and these electors will then meet to elect representatives to the National Assembly.

3. All active citizens, whatever their condition, profession, or tax, can be elected representatives of the nation.

* * *

They shall take the oath *to maintain with all their power the constitution of the kingdom, decreed by the National Constituent Assembly, in the years 1789, 1790, and 1791; and not to propose nor to consent within the course of the legislature to anything which can injure it, and to be in everything faithful to the nation, the law, and the King.*

7. The representatives of the nation are inviolable: they cannot be questioned, accused, nor tried at any time for what they have said, written, or done in the exercise of their functions as representatives.

8. They can, for criminal acts, be seized in the very act or in virtue of a warrant of arrest; but notice shall be given thereof without delay to the Legislative Body; and the prosecution can be continued only after the Legislative Body shall have decided that there is occasion for accusation.

CHAPTER II. OF THE ROYALTY, THE REGENCY, AND THE MINISTERS

Section I. Of the royalty and the King

1. Royalty is indivisible and is delegated hereditarily to the ruling family, from male to male, by order of primogeniture, to the perpetual exclusion of females and their descendants. . . .

2. The person of the King is inviolable and sacred: his only title is *King of the French.*

3. There is no authority[7] in France superior to that of the law; the King reigns only by it and it is only in the name of the law that he can demand obedience.

4. The King, upon his accession to the throne or as soon as he shall have attained his majority, shall take to the nation, in the presence of the Legislative Body, the oath *to be faithful to the nation and the law, to employ all the power which is delegted to him to maintain the constitution decreed by the National Constituent Assembly in the years 1789, 1790, and 1791, and to cause the laws to be executed.*

* * *

6. If the King puts himself at the head of an army and directs the forces thereof against the nation, or if he does not by a formal instrument place himself

---

7. The king's authority derives from the constitution, and not the other way around. Whenever a new monarch is crowned, he is obliged to swear loyalty to the constitution. The king's lands are to be transferred to the nation, and the king is to be supported (given a salary from a civil list) according to the dictates of the National Assembly.

in opposition to any such enterprise which may be conducted in his name, he shall be considered to have abdicated the royalty.

* * *

8. After the express or legal abdication, the King shall be in the class of citizens and can be accused and tried like them for acts subsequent to his abdication.

9. The individual estates which the King possesses upon his accession to the throne are irrevocably united to the domain of the nation: he has the disposal of those which he acquires by personal title; if he does not dispose of them they are likewise united at the end of the reign.

10. The nation provides for the splendor of the throne by a civil list, of which the Legislative Body shall determine the sum at each change of reign for the entire duration of the reign.

* * *

CHAPTER III. OF THE EXERCISE OF THE LEGISLATIVE POWER

Section I. Powers and functions of the National Legislative Assembly[8]

1. The constitution delegates exclusively to the Legislative Body the following powers and functions:

1st. To propose and enact the laws: the King can only invite the Legislative Body to take the matter under consideration;

2d. To fix the public expenditures;

3d. To establish the public taxes, to determine the nature of them, the quota, the duration, and the mode of collection;

4th. To make the apportionment of the direct tax among the departments of the kingdom, to supervise the employment of all the public revenues, and to cause an account of them to be rendered;

5th. To decree the creation or suppression of public offices;

* * *

7th. To permit or forbid the introduction of foreign troops upon French soil and foreign naval forces in the ports of the kingdom;

* * *

2. War can be declared only by a decree of the Legislative Body, rendered upon the formal and indispeasable proposal of the King, and sanctioned by him.

---

8. The legislature has the right to propose and enact laws, to set government revenues and budgets, and to declare war and ratify peace treaties.

In case hostilities are imminent or already begun, or in case of an alliance to sustain or a right to preserve by force of arms, the King shall give notification of it without delay to the Legislative Body and shall make known the causes thereof. If the Legislative Body is in recess the King shall convoke it immediately.

If the Legislative Body decides that war ought not to be made, the King shall take measures immediately to cause the cessation or prevention of all hostilities, the ministers remaining responsible for delays.

If the Legislative Body finds the hostilities already commenced to be a culpable aggression on the part of the ministers or of any other agent of the executive power, the author of the aggression shall be prosecuted criminally.

During the entire course of the war the Legislative Body can require the King to negotiate for peace; and the King is required to yield to this requisition.

As soon as the war shall have ceased the Legislative Body shall fix the period within which the troops raised in excess of the peace footing shall be discharged and the army reduced to its usual condition.

3. The ratification of treaties of peace, alliance, and commerce belongs to the Legislative Body; and no treaty shall have effect except by this ratification.

* * *

Section III. Of the royal sanction

1. The decrees of the Legislative Body are presented to the King, who can refuse his consent to them.[9]

2. In the case where the King refuses his consent, this refusal is only suspensive.

When the two legislatures following that which shall have presented the decree shall have again presented the same decree in the same terms, the King shall be considered to have given the sanction.

3. The consent of the King is expressed upon each decree by this formula signed by the King: *The King consents and will cause it to be executed.*

The suspensive refusal is expressed by this: *The King will examine.*

4. The King is required to express his consent or his refusal upon each decree within two months from the presentation.

5. No decree to which the King has refused his consent can be presented again by the same legislature.

6. The decrees sanctioned by the King and those which shall have been presented by three consecutive legislatures have the force of law, and bear the name and title of *laws*.

7. The following are executed as laws, without being subject to the sanction: The acts of the Legislative Body concerning its constitution in deliberative assembly;

---

9. The monarch's relationship to most legislative matters—when he has any control—is merely suspensive: he can postpone implementation of legislation for two subsequent legislatures.

Its internal police, and that which it is allowed to exercise in the environs which it shall have determined;

The verification of the powers of its members in attendance;

The orders to the absent members;

The convocation of the primary assemblies which are late;

The exercise of the constitutional police over the administrators and the municipal officers;

Questions either of eligibility or of the validity of elections.

In like manner, neither the acts relative to the responsibility of the ministers nor the decrees providing that there is cause for accusation are subject to the sanction.

8. The decrees of the Legislative Body concerning the establishment, the promulgation, and the collection of the public taxes shall bear the name and the title of *laws*. They shall be promulgated and executed without being subject to the sanction, except for the provisions which establish penalties other than fines and pecuniary constraints.

★ ★ ★

CHAPTER IV. OF THE EXERCISE OF THE EXECUTIVE POWER

1. The supreme executive power resides exclusively in the hands of the King.[10]

The King is the supreme head of the general administration of the kingdom; the task of looking after the maintenance of public order and tranquility is confided to him.

The King is the supreme head of the army and navy.

The task of looking after the external security of the kingdom and of maintaining its rights and possessions is delegated to the King.

★ ★ ★

TITLE IV. OF THE PUBLIC FORCE

1. The public force is instituted in order to defend the State against enemies from abroad, and to assure within the maintenance of order and the execution of the laws.

2. It is composed of the army and the navy, of the troops especially intended for internal service, and subsidiarily of the active citizens and their children, in condition to bear arms, registered upon the roll of the national guard.

---

10. The king remains the head of executive matters—"the general administration of the kingdom"—and he is also the supreme head of the army and navy. But insofar as the budgets for all ministries are subject to approval by the legislature, the powers of the king and his ministers are sharply constrained.

3. The national guards form neither a military body nor an institution within the State; they are the citizens themselves summoned to service in the public force.

* * *

TITLE V. OF THE PUBLIC TAXES

1. The public taxes are considered and fixed each year by the Legislative Body and they shall not remain in force beyond the last day of the following session, unless they have been expressly renewed.

2. Under no pretext shall the funds necessary for the discharge of the national debt and the payment of the civil list be refused or suspended.

The compensation of the ministers of the Catholic sect, pensioned, maintained, elected, or appointed in virtue of the decrees of the National Assembly, makes part of the national debt.

TITLE VI. OF THE RELATIONS OF THE FRENCH NATION WITH FOREIGN NATIONS

The French nation renounces the undertaking of any war with a view to making conquests, and will never employ its forces against the liberty of any people.

EDMUND BURKE

FROM *Reflections on the Revolution in France*, 1790

Edmund Burke (1729–1797), though born in Dublin, Ireland, was one of the leading eighteenth-century intellectuals in the British Parliament. When the American colonists bristled over British tax policies in the 1770s, Burke sided with the colonists; he later supported the American independence movement. When the French Revolution broke out, many assumed that Burke would defend it as well. But when the National Assembly wrested power from the monarchy and then attacked the Catholic Church and the nobility, Burke became indignant. When a friend expressed his admiration for the French revolutionaries, Burke replied in November of 1789 with a letter—a very long one—that became one of the classic texts of conservative political thought. Reflections on the Revolution in France (1790) is a powerful defense of social and political traditions, of evolutionary change, and of gentlemanly standards of behavior. Burke was appalled by the violence, social chaos, and destruction of institutions in France, which he largely blamed on Rousseau's Social Contract, *an exercise in creating government from radical theoretical principles.*

Burke has strong intellectual ties to the philosophes. *His request in this letter for "a permanent body" and "an effectual organ" shows the influence of English constitutional thought and Montesquieu's writings, as well as a desire for rational debate and legislation. Despite his affinity for Enlightenment rationality, however, Burke will outline where he differs from the form of Enlightenment thought that the French have enacted. Chief among their errors, according to Burke, are their wholesale abandonment of the old system, which might have worked given the king's concessions after the Fall of the Bastille, and their choice to build a new society from the ground up, incorporating nothing from the past. In Burke's view, the revolutionaries would have been better served by building on preexisting societal and governmental structures, rather than starting anew with no reference to historical precedent.*

What follows is a distillation of Burke's classic work, edited to focus on themes that will likely surface in the game. Burke was a masterful writer, though his precise prose is sometimes difficult for modern readers to decipher. The editors of the following excerpts have sometimes simplified Burke's language (indicated by text within brackets) or otherwise made editorial changes to promote comprehension. For example, Burke argues that we should not worship those who possess lots of money, nor should we punish them merely for being wealthy: "For though hereditary wealth and the rank which goes with it are too much idolized by creeping sycophants and the blind, abject admirers of power, they are too rashly slighted in shallow speculations of the petulant, assuming, shortsighted coxcombs of philosophy." The editors have rewritten this passage in a less glorious, but simpler idiom, as follows: "Too many people grovel before the rich and famous; this is foolish. But it is equally foolish to insist that wealth is of no value, as so many radical philosophers assume."

SOURCE: *Edmund Burke,* Reflections on the Revolution in France, *2nd ed. (London: J. Dodsley, 1790).*

In this preliminary section to his argument, Burke warns about the dangers of the French Revolution.

Dear Sir:

You are pleased to call again, and with some earnestness, for my thoughts on the late proceedings [the Revolution] in France. [My thoughts on the matter] are of too little consequence to be very anxiously either communicated or withheld. My errors, if any, are my own. My reputation alone is to answer for them.

* * *

You see, Sir, that though I do most heartily wish that France may be animated by a spirit of rational liberty [as advocated by the *philosophes*], it is my misfortune to entertain great doubts concerning several material points in your late [writings in support of the French revolutionaries.]

You [French people] might, if you pleased, have profited of our [British] example and have given to your recovered freedom [since the fall of the Bastille] a correspondent dignity. Your privileges, though discontinued, were not lost to memory. Your constitution, it is true, whilst you were out of possession, suffered waste and dilapidation; but you possessed in some parts the walls and in all the basic foundations of a noble and venerable castle. You might have repaired those walls; you might have built on those old foundations. Your constitution was suspended before it was perfected, but you had the elements of a constitution very nearly as good as could be wished.[1] In your old states you possessed that variety of parts corresponding with the various descriptions of which your community was happily composed; you had all that combination and all that opposition of interests; you had that action and counter-action which, in the natural and in the political world, from the reciprocal struggle of discordant powers, draws out the harmony of the universe. These opposed and conflicting interests, which you considered as so great a blemish in your old and in our present constitution interpose a salutary check to all precipitate resolutions. [The Three French "Estates"] render deliberation a matter, not of choice, but of necessity; they make all change a subject of compromise, which naturally begets moderation; they produce temperaments preventing the sore evil of harsh, crude, unqualified reformations [such as the bloodshed of the French Revolution], and rendering all the headlong exertions of arbitrary power, in the few or in the many, forever impracticable. Through that diversity of members and interests [such as voiced by the clergy, nobility, and the commoners], general liberty had as many securities as there were separate views in the several orders, whilst, by [being fused by the force of a powerful monarchy], the separate parts would [remain in a proper balance].[2]

> The French revolutionaries erred in discarding institutions and values whose roots extend deep into the past.

---

1. Burke refers to the historic forms of freedom to which the French understood themselves to be entitled, including the existence of a representative legislative body in the Estates General.

2. Burke means the checks and balances of the old French and English constitutions, but by implication also endorses the "separation of powers" of the executive, judicial, and executive branches of the United States Constitution, adopted just a decade earlier.

You had all these advantages in your ancient states, but you chose to act as if you had never been molded into civil society and had everything to begin anew. You began ill, because you began by despising everything that belonged to you. [Perhaps you had given your monarch too much power, but that did not mean that you had to destroy the entire social and political structure. You could have recovered your ancient traditions, and adapted them to the present.] By following wise examples you would have given new examples of wisdom to the world. You would have rendered the cause of liberty venerable in the eyes of every worthy mind in every nation. You would have shamed despotism from the earth by showing that freedom was not only reconcilable, but, as when well-disciplined it is, auxiliary to law. [And instead of plunging your nation into chaos,] you would have had an unoppressive but productive revenue. You would have had a flourishing commerce to feed it. You would have had a free constitution, a potent monarchy, a disciplined army, a reformed and venerated clergy, a mitigated but spirited nobility to lead your virtue, not to overlay it; you would have had a liberal order of commons to emulate and to recruit that nobility; you would have had a protected, satisfied, laborious, and obedient people, taught to seek and to recognize the happiness that is to be found by virtue in all conditions; in which consists the true moral equality of mankind.

* * *

See what is got by those extravagant and presumptuous speculations [such as Rousseau's preposterous "social contract"] which have taught [the French revolutionaries] to despise all their predecessors, and all their contemporaries, and even to despise themselves until the moment in which they become truly despicable. By following those false lights, France has bought undisguised calamities at a higher price than any nation has purchased the most unequivocal blessings!

Instead, you French revolutionaries have repudiated your own past. And in so doing, you have ruined your nation.

* * *

All other nations have begun the fabric of a new government, or the reformation of an old, by establishing originally or by enforcing with greater exactness some rites or other of religion. All other people have laid the foundations of civil freedom in severer manners and a system of a more austere and masculine morality. France, when she let loose the reins of regal authority, [mocked religious beliefs and rituals and encouraged immorality; all can do as they wish, regardless of the consequences]. This is one of the new principles of equality in France.[3]

* * *

---

3. Burke, though a Protestant, attacks the French revolutionaries for weakening the Catholic Church; he believes that religion promotes virtue and subdues human passions.

[And thus] the French rebel against a mild and lawful monarch [Louis XVI] with more fury, outrage, and insult than ever any people has been known to rise against the most illegal usurper or the most sanguinary tyrant. Their resistance was made to concession, their revolt was from protection, their blow was aimed at a hand holding out graces, favors, and immunities.

[The French revolutionaries] have found their punishment in their success: laws overturned; tribunals subverted; industry without vigor; commerce expiring; the [tax] revenue unpaid, yet the people impoverished; a church pillaged, and a state not relieved; civil and military anarchy made the constitution of the kingdom; everything human and divine sacrificed to the idol of public credit, and national bankruptcy the consequence; and, to crown all, the paper securities of new, precarious, tottering power, the discredited paper securities of impoverished fraud and beggared rapine, held out as a currency for the support of an empire in lieu of the two great recognized species [gold and silver] that represent the lasting, conventional credit of mankind, which disappeared and hid themselves in the earth from whence they came, when the principle of property, whose creatures and representatives they are, was systematically subverted.[4]

Were all these dreadful things necessary? Were they the inevitable results of the desperate struggle of determined patriots, compelled to wade through blood and tumult to the quiet shore of a tranquil and prosperous liberty? No! Nothing like it. The fresh ruins of France, which shock our feelings wherever we can turn our eyes, are not the devastation of civil war; they are the sad but instructive monuments of rash and ignorant counsel [by the radical leaders] in time of profound peace.

The French revolutionaries had no reason to resort to desperate, bloody measures.

* * *

[The revolutionaries] have demolished and laid everything level at their feet. Not one drop of their blood have they shed in the cause of the country they have ruined. They have made no sacrifices to their projects of greater consequence than their shoebuckles,[5] whilst they were imprisoning their king, murdering their fellow citizens, and bathing in tears and plunging in poverty and distress thousands of worthy men and worthy families. Their cruelty has not even been the base result of fear. It has been the effect of their sense of perfect safety, in authorizing

---

4. "Discredited paper securities of impoverished fraud and beggared rapine" refers to *assignats*, the paper notes that the National Assembly legalized as currency, supplementing gold and silver coins and notes redeemable in specie. The *assignats* were valuable insofar as they were funded by the sale of land that the National Assembly had confiscated from the Catholic Church. The Assembly, destitute of funds to run the government, sought to steal it from the Catholic Church, or so Burke suggests.

5. See page 29 in Versailles to Varennes, which mentions the donations of personal wealth, including the buckles from shoes.

The National Assembly of France is the source of the calamity of the French Revolution.

treasons, robberies, rapes, assassinations, slaughters, and burnings throughout their harassed land. But the cause of all was plain from the beginning.

This unforced choice, this fond election of evil, would appear perfectly unaccountable if we did not consider the composition of the National Assembly [which arose through the merger of the Three Estates during the tumultuous summer of 1789]. I do not mean its formal constitution, which, as it now stands, is exceptionable enough, but the materials of which, in a great measure, it is composed, which is of ten thousand times greater consequence than all the formalities in the world.

* * *

After I had read over the list of the persons and descriptions elected into the [Third Estate], nothing which they afterwards did could appear astonishing. Among them, indeed, I saw some of known rank, some of shining talents; but of any practical experience in the state, not one man was to be found. The best were only men of theory [that is, philosophical speculation].

* * *

Lawyers predominated in the Assembly, and lawyers are poor lawmakers.

I found the representation for the Third Estate composed of six hundred persons.[6] They were equal in number to the representatives of both the other orders. If the orders were to act separately, the number would not, beyond the consideration of the expense, be of much moment. But when it became apparent that the three orders were to be melted down into one, the policy and necessary effect of this numerous representation became obvious. A very small desertion from either of the other two orders must throw the power of both into the hands of the third. In fact, the whole power of the state was soon resolved into that body. Its due composition became therefore of infinitely the greater importance.

Judge, Sir, of my surprise when I found that a very great proportion of the Assembly (a majority, I believe, of the members who attended) was composed of practitioners in the law. It was composed, not of distinguished magistrates, who had given pledges to their country of their science, prudence, and integrity; not of leading advocates, the glory of the bar; not of renowned professors in universities— but for the far greater part, as it must in such a number, of the inferior, unlearned,

---

6. Here, Burke lays out his argument that the men who made up the National Assembly were ill-suited for the work that they had to do, with little experience in administration or governing, and that, in fact, the very composition of the Third Estate's representatives is the source of the conflict and the origin of the disaster that Burke describes. A few representatives are learned men of renown, but the majority are grasping small-town lawyers, without reputation or experience, and with local, not national, vision.

mechanical, merely instrumental members of the profession. There were distinguished exceptions, but the general composition was of obscure provincial advocates, of stewards of petty local jurisdictions, country attorneys, notaries, and the whole train of the ministers of municipal litigation, the fomenters and conductors of the petty war of village vexation. From the moment I read the list, I saw distinctly, and very nearly as it has happened, all that was to follow.

* * *

Who could flatter himself that these men, suddenly and, as it were, by enchantment snatched from the humblest rank of subordination, would not be intoxicated with their unprepared greatness [as delegates to the National Assembly of France]? Who could conceive that men who are habitually meddling, daring, subtle, active, of litigious dispositions and unquiet minds would easily fall back into their old condition of obscure contention and laborious, low, unprofitable chicane? Who could doubt but that, at any expense to the state, of which they understood nothing, they must pursue their private interests, which they understand but too well?

* * *

[In addition to the local lawyers and law professors were a group of delegates who belonged to the faculty of medicine, and still others whose only skill was in selling stock and manipulating financial markets.] To these were joined men of other descriptions, from whom as little knowledge of, or attention to, the interests of a great state was to be expected, and as little regard to the stability of any institution; men formed to be instruments, not controls. Such in general was the composition of [the Third Estate] in the National Assembly, in which was scarcely to be perceived the slightest traces of what we call the natural landed interest of the country, [people whose families had long owned landed estates].

* * *

The National Assembly, since the destruction of the orders, has no fundamental law, no strict convention, no respected usage to restrain it. Instead of finding themselves obliged to conform to a fixed constitution, they have a power to make a constitution which shall conform to their designs. Nothing in heaven or upon earth can serve as a control on them. What ought to be the heads, the hearts, the dispositions that are qualified or that dare, not only to make laws under a fixed constitution, but at one heat to strike out a totally new constitution for a great kingdom, and in every part of it, from the monarch on the throne to the vestry of a parish? But—"fools rush in where angels fear to tread." In such a state of unbounded power for undefined and undefinable purposes, the evil of a moral and almost physical inaptitude of the man to the function must be the greatest we can conceive to happen in the management of human affairs.

The National Assembly has too much power, with no other institutions to check that power.

Having considered the composition of the Third Estate as it stood in its original frame, I took a view of the representatives of the clergy. There, too, it appeared that full as little regard was had to the general security of property or to the aptitude of the deputies for the public purposes, in the principles of their election. That election [of the delegates for the clergy] was so contrived as to send a very large proportion of mere country curates [priests] to the great and arduous work of new-modeling a state: men who never had seen the state so much as in a picture—men who knew nothing of the world beyond the bounds of an obscure village; who, immersed in hopeless poverty, could regard all property, whether secular or ecclesiastical, with no other eye than that of envy; among whom must be many who, for the smallest hope of the meanest dividend in plunder, would readily join in any attempts upon a body of wealth in which they could hardly look to have any share except in a general scramble.

* * *

This preponderating weight, being added to the force of the body of chicane [outrageous acts among members of the Third Estate], completed that momentum of ignorance, rashness, presumption, and lust of plunder, which nothing has been able to resist.

The revolutionaries in the National Assembly foolishly endorse equality, but men are not equal.

Believe me, Sir, those who attempt to level [to pull down those who are above you], never equalize. In all societies, consisting of various descriptions of citizens, some description must be uppermost. The levelers, therefore, only change and pervert the natural order of things; they load the edifice of society by setting up in the air what the solidity of the structure requires to be on the ground. The association of tailors and carpenters [who run the sections of Paris and thus rule Paris itself, cannot possibly be equal to the task that they have stolen from rightful leaders, because tailors and carpenters weren't meant to rule.]

The Chancellor of France, at the opening of the [Estates General], said, in a tone of oratorical flourish, that all occupations were honorable. If he meant only that no honest employment was disgraceful, he would not have gone beyond the truth. But in asserting that anything is honorable, we imply some distinction in its favor. The occupation of a hairdresser or of a working tallow-chandler cannot be a matter of honor to any person—to say nothing of a number of other more servile employments. Such descriptions of men ought not to suffer oppression from the state; but the state suffers oppression if such as they, either individually or collectively, are permitted to rule. In this you think you are combating prejudice, but you are at war with nature.[7]

* * *

7. Burke insists that government requires men of talent and virtue, and the men who are seizing the reins of power delude themselves, because of self-interest, into thinking that anyone can do this job. It ought to be difficult to rule, something that is only open to men of demonstrated virtue and valor.

Do not imagine that I wish to confine power, authority, and distinction to blood and names and titles. No, Sir. There is no qualification for government but virtue and wisdom, actual or presumptive. Wherever they are actually found, they have, in whatever state, condition, profession, or trade, the passport of Heaven to human place and honor. Woe to the country which would madly and impiously reject the service of the talents and virtues, civil, military, or religious, that are given to grace and to serve it.

* * *

Woe to that country, too, that, passing into the opposite extreme, considers a low education, a mean contracted view of things, a sordid, mercenary occupation as a preferable title to command.

If civil society be made for the advantage of man, all the advantages for which it is made become his right. It is an institution of beneficence; and law itself is only beneficence acting by a rule. Men have a right to live by that rule; they have a right to do justice, as between their fellows, whether their fellows are in public function or in ordinary occupation. They have a right to the fruits of their industry and to the means of making their industry fruitful. They have a right to the acquisitions of their parents, to the nourishment and improvement of their off-spring, to instruction in life, and to consolation in death. Whatever each man can separately do, without trespassing upon others, he has a right to do for himself; and he has a right to a fair portion of all which society, with all its combinations of skill and force, can do in his favor. In this partnership all men have equal rights, but not to equal things. He that has but five shillings in the partnership has as good a right to it as he that has five hundred pounds has to his larger proportion. But he has not a right to an equal dividend in the product of the joint stock; and as to the share of power, authority, and direction which each individual ought to have in the management of the state, that I must deny to be amongst the direct original rights of man in civil society; for I have in my contemplation the civil social man, and no other. It is a thing to be settled by convention.[8]

> There is no "natural right" to equality: *redistributing property to achieve equality is wrong.*

---

8. This is political theory of Thomas Hobbes and John Locke. It recognizes that men have a difficult time restraining their desires, which must therefore be restrained by government. Unlike Locke, Burke insists on the particularity of nations and, accordingly, on the importance of tradition. Though it would be impossible for any civil society to function without restraints, the restraints that are necessary for each nation will vary—those in England may differ widely from those in France. Thus, it is impossible to determine in the abstract what rights and restraints are appropriate to any particular society. In short, natural rights philosophy fails to recognize the particular and fundamental nature of restraint in governing men's passions. Abstract principles cannot cover all possible conditions, nor can one calculate in advance all human motivations.

Government is needed to subdue men's passions—including their greed for the property *of others*.

Government is not made in virtue of natural rights, which may and do exist in total independence of it, and exist in much greater clearness and in a much greater degree of abstract perfection; but their abstract perfection is their practical defect. By having a right to everything they want everything. Government is a contrivance of human wisdom to provide for human wants [i.e., needs]. Men have a right that these wants should be provided for by this wisdom. Among these wants is to be reckoned the want, out of civil society, of a sufficient restraint upon their passions. Society requires not only that the passions of individuals should be subjected, but that even in the mass and body, as well as in the individuals, the inclinations of men should frequently be thwarted, their will controlled, and their passions brought into subjection.

* * *

What is the use of discussing a man's abstract right to food or medicine? The question is upon the method of procuring and administering them. In that delib-

The institutions of government emerge over time; they cannot be constructed from philosophical principles.

eration I shall always advise to call in the aid of the farmer and the physician rather than the professor of metaphysics.

The science of constructing a commonwealth, or renovating it, or reforming it, is, like every other experimental science, not to be taught *a priori* [starting from a clean slate]. Nor is it a short experience that can instruct us in that practical science, because the real effects of moral causes are not always immediate.

* * *

The science of government being therefore so practical in itself and intended for such practical purposes—a matter which requires experience, and even more experience than any person can gain in his whole life, however sagacious and observing he may be—it is with infinite caution that any man ought to venture upon pulling down an edifice which has answered in any tolerable degree for ages the common purposes of society, or on building it up again without having models and patterns of approved utility before his eyes.[9]

The nature of man is intricate; the objects of society are of the greatest possible complexity; and, therefore, no simple disposition or direction of power

---

9. The particular nature of each government and the need to look at specifics means that governments must be constructed on historical foundations, not invented from scratch or derived from fanciful ideas about the nature of humanity. The art of government is a practical one that requires experience and judgment—something that the deputies had in short supply—rather than abstract theorizing. Moreover, it may take time for the results of political experiments to become known. Thus, history, not philosophy, provides the foundation for good governments.

can be suitable either to man's nature or to the quality of his affairs. When I hear the simplicity of contrivance aimed at and boasted of in any new political constitutions, I am at no loss to decide that the artificers are grossly ignorant of their trade or totally negligent of their duty.

* * *

In France, you are now in the crisis of a revolution and in the transit from one form of government to another. . . . This sort of people are so taken up with their theories about the rights of man that they have totally forgotten his nature.

* * *

The arrest of the king [when he and his family were removed from Versailles and forcibly brought to the Tuileries palace in Paris], my dear Sir, was not the triumph of France. I must believe that, as a nation, it overwhelmed you with shame and horror.

> *The National Assembly, while depriving the king of his rights, is controlled by a murderous gang—the crowd of Paris.*

* * *

With a compelled appearance of deliberation, [the National Assembly votes] under the dominion of a stern necessity. They sit in the heart, as it were, of a foreign republic: they have their residence in a city whose constitution has emanated neither from the charter of their king nor from their legislative power. There they are surrounded by an army not raised either by the authority of their crown or by their command, and which, if they should order to dissolve itself, would instantly dissolve them. There they sit, after a gang of assassins, [the volatile and unthinking crowds of Paris and their section leaders], had driven away some hundreds of the members, whilst those who held the same moderate principles, with more patience or better hope, continued every day exposed to outrageous insults and murderous threats. There a majority, sometimes real, sometimes pretended, captive itself, compels a captive king to issue as royal edicts, at third hand, the polluted nonsense of their most licentious and giddy coffeehouses. It is notorious that all their measures are decided before they are debated. It is beyond doubt that, under the terror of the bayonet and the lamppost and the torch to their houses, they are obliged to adopt all the crude and desperate measures suggested by clubs composed of a monstrous medley of all conditions, tongues, and nations.

* * *

The National Assembly, their organ, acts before them the farce of deliberation with as little decency as liberty. They act like the comedians of a fair before a riotous audience; they act amidst the tumultuous cries of a mixed mob of ferocious men, and of women lost to shame, who, according to their insolent fancies, direct, control, applaud, explode them, and sometimes mix and take their seats amongst them, domineering over them with a strange mixture of servile petulance and proud, presumptuous authority. As they have inverted order in all things, the gallery is in the place of the house. This assembly, which overthrows kings and kingdoms, has not even the physiognomy and aspect of a grave legislative body.... They have a power given to them, like that of the evil principle, to subvert and destroy, but none to construct, except such machines as may be fitted for further subversion and further destruction.

Marie Antoinette is a good woman and queen, yet the revolutionaries treat her horribly. It is now sixteen or seventeen years since I saw the queen of France, then the dauphiness, at Versailles, and surely never lighted on this orb, which she hardly seemed to touch, a more delightful vision. I saw her just above the horizon, decorating and cheering the elevated sphere she just began to move in—glittering like the morning star, full of life and splendor and joy.

* * *

Little ... did I dream that I should have lived to see such disasters fallen upon her in a nation of gallant men, in a nation of men of honor and of cavaliers. I thought ten thousand swords must have leaped from their scabbards to avenge even a look that threatened her with insult. But the age of chivalry is gone....

Never, never more shall we behold that generous loyalty to rank and sex, that proud submission, that dignified obedience, that subordination of the heart which kept alive, even in servitude itself, the spirit of an exalted freedom.... It is gone, that sensibility of principle, that chastity of honor which felt a stain like a wound, which inspired courage whilst it mitigated ferocity, which ennobled whatever it touched, and under which vice itself lost half its evil by losing all its grossness.[10]

On this scheme of things, a king is but a man, a queen is but a woman; a woman is but an animal, and an animal not of the highest order. All homage paid to the sex in general as such, and without distinct views, is to be regarded as romance and folly. Regicide, and parricide, and sacrilege are but fictions of superstition, corrupting jurisprudence by destroying its simplicity. The murder of a king, or a queen, or a bishop, or a father are only common homicide; and if the people are by any

---

10. In this famous passage, Burke's rapturous recollection of Marie Antoinette and of the value of chivalry may strike contemporary readers as absurd. But this argument helps prepare Burke's larger point, and it merits a sympathetic reading. Burke believes that part of what brings meaning to human life is the very inequality attacked by the revolution. Burke's fear is that an oppressive attachment to equality destroys any and all distinctions, and that these distinctions—properly understood and properly limited—bring meaning and beauty not just to the powerful, but to all of society. The capture of the king and his forcible return to Paris in October, 1789, laid bare the underlying violence of the Revolution, and invite other monarchs of Europe to become tyrants in response.

chance or in any way gainers by it, a sort of homicide much the most pardonable, and into which we ought not to make too severe a scrutiny.

We are but too apt to consider things in the state in which we find them, without sufficiently adverting to the causes by which they have been produced and possibly may be upheld. Nothing is more certain than that our manners, our civilization, and all the good things which are connected with manners and with civilization have, in this European world of ours, depended for ages upon two principles and were, indeed, the result of both combined: I mean the spirit of a gentleman and the spirit of religion. The nobility and the clergy, the one by profession, the other by patronage, kept learning in existence, even in the midst of arms and confusions, and whilst governments were rather in their causes than formed. Learning paid back what it received to nobility and to priesthood, and paid it [richly], by enlarging their ideas and by furnishing their minds.

The two pillars of society are religion and a gentlemanly spirit: the Assembly wages war on both.

[By contrast] already there appears a poverty of conception, a coarseness, and a vulgarity in all the proceedings of the National Assembly and of all their instructors. Their liberty is not liberal. Their science is presumptuous ignorance. Their humanity is savage and brutal.

* * *

If it could have been made clear to me that the king and queen of France (those I mean who were such before the triumph [of the revolutionaries]) were inexorable and cruel tyrants, that they had formed a deliberate scheme for massacring the National Assembly (I think I have seen something like the latter insinuated in certain publications), I should think their captivity [in the Tuileries palace in Paris to be] just.

King Louis XVI is being treated unfairly.

* * *

But to degrade and insult a man as the worst of criminals and afterwards to trust him in your highest concerns [as the monarch according to the new constitution]—as a faithful, honest, and zealous servant is not consistent to reasoning, nor prudent in policy, nor safe in practice. Those who could make such an appointment must be guilty of a more flagrant breach of trust than any they have yet committed against the people. As this is the only crime in which your leading politicians could have acted inconsistently, I conclude that there is no sort of ground for these horrid insinuations. I think no better of all the other calumnies.

The British are properly wary of newfangled ideas; the French have foolishly fallen for crazy schemes such as those by Rousseau.

Thanks to our sullen resistance to innovation [in Britain], thanks to the cold sluggishness of our national character, we still bear the stamp of our forefathers. We have not (as I conceive) lost the generosity and dignity of thinking of the fourteenth century, nor as yet have we subtilized ourselves into savages.

We are not the converts of Rousseau; we are not the disciples of Voltaire.

* * *

Atheists are not our preachers; madmen are not our lawgivers. We know that we have made no discoveries, and we think that no discoveries are to be made in morality, nor many in the great principles of government, nor in the ideas of liberty, which were understood long before we were born, altogether as well as they will be after the grace has heaped its mold upon our presumption and the silent tomb shall have imposed its law on our pert loquacity.

* * *

We preserve the whole of our feelings still native and entire, unsophisticated by pedantry and infidelity. We have real hearts of flesh and blood beating in our bosoms. We fear God; we look up with awe to kings, with affection to parliaments, with duty to magistrates, with reverence to priests, and with respect to nobility. Why? Because when such ideas are brought before our minds, it is natural to be so affected; because all other feelings are false and spurious and tend to corrupt our minds, to vitiate our primary morals, to render us unfit for rational liberty.

* * *

Religion is the proper foundation of civil society. We know, and what is better, we feel inwardly, that religion is the basis of civil society and the source of all good and of all comfort. In England we are so convinced of this, that there is no rust of superstition with which the accumulated absurdity of the human mind might have crusted it over in the course of ages, that ninety-nine in a hundred of the people of England would not prefer to impiety. We shall never be such fools as to call in an enemy to the substance of any system to remove its corruptions, to supply its defects, or to perfect its construction. If our religious tenets should ever want a further elucidation, we shall not call on atheism to explain them.

* * *

We know, and it is our pride to know, that man is by his constitution a religious animal; that atheism is against, not only our reason, but our instincts; and that it cannot prevail long. But if, in the moment of riot and in a drunken delirium from the hot spirit drawn out of the alembic [distillation process] of hell, which in France is now so furiously boiling, we should uncover our nakedness by throwing off that Christian religion which has hitherto been our boast and comfort, and one great source of civilization amongst us and amongst many other nations, we are apprehensive (being well aware that the mind will not endure a void) that some uncouth, pernicious, and degrading superstition might take place of it.

* * *

Society is indeed a contract [but not like the one we make in buying goods or services].[11] It is to be looked on with other reverence, because it is not a partnership in things subservient only to the gross animal existence of a temporary and perishable nature. It is a partnership in all science; a partnership in all art; a partnership in every virtue and in all perfection. As the ends of such a partnership cannot be obtained in many generations, it becomes a partnership not only between those who are living, but between those who are living, those who are dead, and those who are to be born. Each contract of each particular state is but a clause in the great primeval contract of eternal society, linking the lower with the higher natures, connecting the visible and invisible world, according to a fixed compact sanctioned by the inviolable oath which holds all physical and all moral natures, each in their appointed place. This law is not subject to the will of those who by an obligation above them, and infinitely superior, are bound to submit their will to that law.

The state is a contract that transcends human desires; it is far more glorious than the "social contract" espoused by Rousseau.

[God] who gave our nature to be perfected by our virtue willed also the necessary means of its perfection. He willed therefore the state—He willed its connection with the source and original archetype of all perfection

* * *

I hope we shall never be so totally lost to all sense of the duties imposed upon us by the law of social union as, upon any pretext of public service, to confiscate the goods of a single unoffending citizen.[12]

The state must preserve property, a bulwark to freedom.

* * *

But this act of seizure of property, it seems, is a judgment in law, and not a confiscation. They have, it seems, found out in the academies of the Palais Royal [where crowds gathered to debate radical ideas, without police control] and the

11. Burke explains that religion fills a basic human need and provides a check on unbridled self-interest. Although he endorses Protestantism, he warns that the destruction of the Catholic Church in France portends disaster: in the absence of settled religious institutions, new and dangerous beliefs can arise, including adherence to new ideas that break down social cohesion and damage society. Rousseau does not entirely disagree with Burke on the necessity of religion; but where Burke emphasizes religion as a force for restraining behavior, Rousseau sees it as the embodiment of community sentiment. Compare Burke's views here to Rousseau's views on religion in the last chapter of *The Social Contract*.

12. Here Burke alludes to the National Assembly's unprecedented confiscation of property from the nobility and various Church entities, acts that he compares with the punishments levied by victorious powers on those they have defeated in war. The Assembly's theft of the property of others, Burke contends, shows what happens when there is no recourse to moral traditions or past law.

The Assembly claims that the Catholic Church did not own the land the Assembly confiscated because the Church is a fictitious person and only persons can own land. Burke disagrees.

Jacobins that certain men had no right to the possessions which they held under law, usage, the decisions of courts, and the accumulated prescription of a thousand years. They say that [church bodies] are fictitious persons, creatures of the state, whom at pleasure they may destroy, and of course limit and modify in every particular; that the goods they possess are not properly theirs but belong to the state which created the fiction; and we are therefore not to trouble ourselves with what they may suffer in their natural feelings and natural persons on account of what is done toward them in this their constructive character. Of what import is it under what names you injure men and deprive them of the just emoluments of a profession, in which they were not only permitted but encouraged by the state to engage, and upon the supposed certainty of which emoluments they had formed the plan of their lives, contracted debts, and led multitudes to an entire dependence upon them?

You do not imagine, Sir, that I am going to compliment this miserable distinction of persons with any long discussion. The arguments of tyranny are as contemptible as its force is dreadful. Had not your confiscators, by their early crimes, obtained a power which secures indemnity to all the crimes of which they have since been guilty or that they can commit, it is not the syllogism of the logician, but the lash of the executioner, that would have refuted a sophistry which becomes an accomplice of theft and murder. The sophistic tyrants of Paris are loud in their declamations against the departed regal tyrants, who in former ages have vexed the world. They are thus bold, because they are safe from the dungeons and iron cages of their old masters.

* * *

Many of those stealing land from the nobility and the Catholic Church are the newly rich businessmen and financiers.

[The new men of monied wealth—the *bourgeoisie*—have directed the fury of the poor of Paris against the Catholic Church and the nobility.] All the envy against wealth and power was artificially directed against other descriptions of riches. On what other principle than that which I have stated can we account for an appearance so extraordinary and unnatural as that of the ecclesiastical possessions, which had stood so many successions of ages and shocks of civil violences, and were girded at once by justice and by prejudice, being applied to the payment of debts comparatively recent, invidious, and contracted by a decried and subverted government?[13] Nothing can lead more to the true spirit of the Assembly, which sits for public

---

13. The National Assembly, made up of representatives from these classes who are envious and inexperienced, have acted barbarously by stealing Church land. While the Church was not the source of the national debt and had acted to help the situation, the Assembly was committed to confiscating their land, proving its hostility and greed.

confiscation, with its new equity and its new morality, than an attention to their proceeding with regard to this debt of the clergy. The body of confiscators, true to that monied interest for which they were false to every other, have found the clergy competent to incur a legal debt. Of course, they declared them legally entitled to the property which their power of incurring the debt and mortgaging the estate implied, recognizing the rights of those persecuted citizens in the very act in which they were thus grossly violated.

* * *

If I recollect rightly, Aristotle observes that a democracy has many striking points of resemblance with a tyranny. Of this I am certain, that in a democracy the majority of the citizens is capable of exercising the most cruel oppressions upon the minority whenever strong divisions prevail in that kind of polity, as they often must; and that oppression of the minority will extend to far greater numbers and will be carried on with much greater fury than can almost ever be apprehended from the dominion of a single scepter [ruler]. In such a popular persecution, individual sufferers are in a much more deplorable condition than in any other. Under a cruel prince they have the balmy compassion of mankind to assuage the smart of their wounds; they have the plaudits of the people to animate their generous constancy under their sufferings; but those who are subjected to wrong under multitudes are deprived of all external consolation. They seem deserted by mankind, overpowered by a conspiracy of their whole species.

Democracies often oppress those who are in the minority.

Your government in France, though usually, and I think justly, reputed the best of the unqualified or ill-qualified monarchies, was still full of abuses. These abuses accumulated in a length of time, as they must accumulate in every monarchy not under the constant inspection of a popular representative. But the question is not now of the vices of that monarchy, but of its existence. Is it, then, true that the French government was such as to be incapable or undeserving of reform, so that it was of absolute necessity that the whole fabric should be at once pulled down and the area cleared for the erection of a theoretic, experimental edifice in its place? All France was of a different opinion in the beginning of the year 1789. The instructions to the representatives to the Estates-General, from every district in that kingdom, were filled with projects for the reformation of that government without the remotest suggestion of a design to destroy it.

The French monarchy had its faults, but it could have been reformed.

[Insofar as I could tell, the French nobility behaved toward the lower classes] with good nature and with something more nearly approaching to familiarity than is generally practiced with us in the intercourse between the higher and lower ranks of life. To strike any person, even in the most abject condition, was a thing in a manner unknown and would be highly disgraceful. Instances of other ill-treatment of the humble part

The French nobility, too, were not generally oppressive or cruel: they should not have been targeted for abuse.

of the community were rare; and as to attacks made upon the property or the personal liberty of the commons, I never heard of any whatsoever from them; nor, whilst the laws were in vigor under the ancient government, would such tyranny in subjects have been permitted. As men of landed estates, I had no fault to find with their conduct, though much to reprehend and much to wish changed in many of the old tenures.

* * *

There might be exceptions, but certainly they were exceptions only. I have no reason to believe that in these respects the landed noblesse of France were worse than the landed gentry of this country, certainly in no respect more vexatious than the landholders, not noble, of their own nation. In cities the nobility had no manner of power, in the country very little. You know, Sir, that much of the civil government, and the police in the most essential parts, was not in the hands of that nobility which presents itself first to our consideration. The revenue, the system and collection of which were the most grievous parts of the French government, was not administered by the men of the sword, nor were they answerable for the vices of its principle or the vexations, where any such existed, in its management.

* * *

All this violent cry against the nobility I take to be a mere work of art. To be honored and even privileged by the laws, opinions, and inveterate usages of our country, growing out of the prejudice of ages, has nothing to provoke horror and indignation in any man. . . . Nobility is a graceful ornament to the civil order. It is the Corinthian capital of polished society. *Omnes boni nobilitati semper favemus*[14] was the saying of a wise and good man. It is indeed one sign of a liberal and benevolent mind to incline to it with some sort of partial propensity. He feels no ennobling principle in his own heart who wishes to level all the artificial institutions which have been adopted for giving a body to opinion, and permanence to fugitive esteem. It is a sour, malignant, envious disposition, without taste for the reality or for any image or representation of virtue, that sees with joy the unmerited fall of what had long flourished in splendor and in honor. . . . Your noblesse did not deserve punishment; but to degrade is to punish.

* * *

The Catholic clergy, too, did not deserve to be attacked by mobs—or by the National Assembly.

From the general style of your late publications of all sorts one would be led to believe that your clergy in France were a sort of monsters, a horrible composition of superstition, ignorance, sloth, fraud, avarice, and tyranny. But is this true? Is it true that they [Catholic

---

14. Cicéro: Those who are good regard the nobility favorably.

officials] were daily renewing invasions on the civil power, troubling the domestic quiet of their country, and rendering the operations of its government feeble and precarious? Is it true that the clergy of our times have pressed down the laity with an iron hand and were in all places lighting up the fires of a savage persecution? Did they by every fraud endeavor to increase their estates? Did they use to exceed the due demands on estates that were their own? Or, rigidly screwing up right into wrong, did they convert a legal claim into a vexatious extortion?[15]

* * *

In short, Sir, it seems to me that this new ecclesiastical establishment [the Civil Constitution of the Clergy] is intended only to be temporary and preparatory to the utter abolition, under any of its forms, of the Christian religion, whenever the minds of men are prepared for this last stroke against it, by the accomplishment of the plan for bringing its ministers into universal contempt. They who will not believe that the philosophical fanatics who guide in these matters have long entertained such a design are utterly ignorant of their character and proceedings. These enthusiasts do not scruple to avow their opinion that a state can subsist without any religion better than with one, and that they are able to supply the place of any good which may be in it by a project of their own—namely, by a sort of education they have imagined, founded in a knowledge of the physical wants of men, progressively carried to an enlightened self-interest which, when well understood, they tell us, will identify with an interest more enlarged and public. The scheme of this education has been long known. Of late they distinguish it (as they have got an entirely new nomenclature of technical terms) by the name of a Civic Education.

* * *

I can never consider this Assembly as anything else than a voluntary association of men who have availed themselves of circumstances to seize upon the power of the state. They have not the sanction and authority of the character under which they first met [as the three Estates of the Estates General in 1789]. They have assumed another of a very different nature and have completely altered and inverted all the relations in which they originally stood. They do not hold the authority they exercise under

The National Assembly has seized for itself the power of the state.

---

15. Burke insists that the French officers of the Catholic Church, like the French monarchy and nobility, were no more vice-ridden or evil than any other groups of men. If they had been, it would perhaps be reasonable to target them. As it is, the revolutionaries are using the supposed guilt of the clergy to destroy religion rather than to reform an actual problem. According to Burke, the power-hungry deputies to the National Assembly seek to destroy all other privileges in order to add to their own power. These men, not the ones that they are attacking, are the true tyrants.

any constitutional law of the state. They have departed from the instructions of the people by whom they were sent, which instructions, as the Assembly did not act in virtue of any ancient usage or settled law, were the sole source of their authority. The most considerable of their acts have not been done by great majorities; and in this sort of near divisions, which carry only the constructive authority of the whole, strangers will consider reasons as well as resolutions.

View this new executive officer on the side of his political capacity, as he acts under the orders of the National Assembly. . . . In France, the king is no more the fountain of honor than he is the fountain of justice. All rewards, all distinctions are in other hands. Those who serve the king can be actuated by no natural motive but fear—by a fear of everything except their master. His functions of internal coercion are as odious as those which he exercises in the department of justice. If relief is to be given to any municipality, the Assembly gives it. If troops are to be sent to reduce them to obedience to the Assembly, the king is to execute the order; and upon every occasion he is to be spattered over with the blood of his people. He has no negative; yet his name and authority is used to enforce every harsh decree. Nay, he must concur in the butchery of those who shall attempt to free him from his imprisonment or show the slightest attachment to his person or to his ancient authority.

The new constitution of France has deprived the king of nearly all of his time-honored powers.

To a person who takes a view of the whole, the strength of Paris, thus formed, will appear a system of general weakness. It is boasted that the geometrical policy has been adopted, that all local ideas should be sunk, and that the people should no longer be Gascons, Picards, Bretons, Normans, but Frenchmen, with one country, one heart, and one Assembly. But instead of being all Frenchmen, the greater likelihood is that the inhabitants of that region will shortly have no country. No man ever was attached by a sense of pride, partiality, or real affection to a description of square measurement.

The elimination of the traditional French provinces and their replacement by "departments" is an outrage.

* * *

We begin our public affections in our families. No cold relation is a zealous citizen. We pass on to our neighborhoods and our habitual provincial connections. These are inns and resting places. Such divisions of our country as have been formed by habit, and not by a sudden jerk of authority, were so many little images of the great country in which the heart found something which it could fill. The love to the whole is not extinguished by this subordinate partiality. Perhaps it is a sort of elemental training to those higher and more large regards by which alone men come to be affected, as with their own concern, in the prosperity of a kingdom so extensive as that of France. In that general territory itself, as in the old name of provinces, the citizens are interested from old prejudices and unreasoned habits, and not on account of the geometric properties of its figure. The power and preeminence of Paris does certainly press down and hold these republics together as long as it lasts. But, for the reasons I have already given you, I think it cannot last very long.[16]

* * *

It is known that armies have hitherto yielded a very precarious and uncertain obedience to any senate or popular authority; and they will least of all yield it to an assembly which is only to have a continuance of two years. The officers must totally lose the characteristic disposition of military men if they see with perfect submission and due admiration the dominion of pleaders. . . . In the weakness of one kind of authority, and in the fluctuation of all, the officers of an army will remain for some time mutinous and full of faction until some popular general, who understands the art of conciliating the soldiery, and who possesses the true spirit of command, shall draw the eyes of all men upon himself. Armies will obey him on his personal account. There is no other way of securing military obedience in this state of things. But the moment in which that event shall happen, the person who really commands the army is your master—the master (that is little) of your king, the master of your Assembly, the master of your whole republic.

The new government lacks an effective army.

* * *

But what is liberty without wisdom and without virtue? It is the greatest of all possible evils; for it is folly, vice, and madness, without tuition or restraint. Those who know what virtuous liberty is cannot bear to see it disgraced by incapable heads on account of their having high-sounding words in their mouths. Grand, swelling sentiments of liberty I am sure I do not despise. They warm the heart; they enlarge and liberalize our minds; they animate our courage in a time of conflict. Old as I am, I read the fine raptures of Lucan [first-century Roman poet] and Corneille [seventeenth-century French playwright] with pleasure. Neither do I wholly condemn the little arts and devices of popularity. They facilitate the carrying of many points of moment; they keep the people together; they refresh the mind in its exertions; and they diffuse occasional gaiety over the severe brow of moral freedom. Every politician ought to sacrifice to the graces, and to join compliance with reason. But in such an undertaking as that in France, all these subsidiary sentiments and artifices are of little avail. To make a government requires no great prudence. Settle the seat of power, teach obedience, and the work is done. To give freedom is still more easy. It

The revolution extols liberty; but liberty untampered by wisdom and virtue is madness.

---

16. Burke contends that the new rational construction of departments destroys the natural affections people have toward their own locality. By nature, we love our traditional identities, not a geometrically defined area. The law attempts to rationalize, but like the Assembly, it forgets history, tradition, and the real social allegiances that make people's lives meaningful.

is not necessary to guide; it only requires to let go the rein. But to form a free government, that is, to temper together these opposite elements of liberty and restraint in one consistent work, requires much thought, deep reflection, a sagacious, powerful, and combining mind. This I do not find in those who take the lead in the National Assembly. Perhaps they are not so miserably deficient as they appear. I rather believe it. It would put them below the common level of human understanding. But when the leaders choose to make themselves bidders at an auction of popularity, their talents, in the construction of the state, will be of no service. They will become flatterers instead of legislators, the instruments, not the guides, of the people. If any of them should happen to propose a scheme of liberty, soberly limited and defined with proper qualifications, he will be immediately outbid by his competitors who will produce something more splendidly popular. Suspicions will be raised of his fidelity to his cause. Moderation will be stigmatized as the virtue of cowards, and compromise as the prudence of traitors, until, in hopes of preserving the credit which may enable him to temper and moderate, on some occasions, the popular leader is obliged to become active in propagating doctrines and establishing powers that will afterwards defeat any sober purpose at which he ultimately might have aimed.

I do not deny that, among an infinite number of acts of violence and folly, some good may have been done. They who destroy everything certainly will remove some grievance. They who make everything new have a chance that they may establish something beneficial. To give them credit for what they have done in virtue of the authority they have usurped, or which can excuse them in the crimes by which that authority has been acquired, it must appear that the same things could not have been accomplished without producing such a revolution. Most

The many acts of the National Assembly are not all bad, but nearly so.

assuredly they might, because almost every one of the regulations made by them which is not very equivocal was either in the cession of the king, voluntarily made at the meeting of the states, or in the concurrent instructions to the orders. Some usages have been abolished on just grounds, but they were such that if they had stood as they were to all eternity, they would little detract from the happiness and prosperity of any state. The improvements of the National Assembly are superficial, their errors fundamental.

. . . I have little to recommend my opinions but long observation and much impartiality. They come from one who has been no tool of power, no flatterer of

A lifelong foe of tyranny, Burke hopes that people will perceive its presence in the French National Assembly.

greatness; and who in his last acts does not wish to belie the tenor of his life. They come from one almost the whole of whose public exertion has been a struggle for the liberty of others; from one in whose breast no anger, durable or vehement, has ever been kindled but by what he considered as tyranny; and who snatches from his share in the endeavors which are used by good men to discredit opulent oppression the hours he has employed on your affairs; and who in so doing persuades himself he has not departed from his usual office; they come from one who desires honors, distinctions, and emoluments but little, and who expects them not at all; who has no contempt for fame, and no fear of obloquy; who shuns contention, though he will hazard an opinion; from one who wishes to preserve consistency, but who would preserve consistency by varying his means to secure the unity of his end, and, when the equipoise [balance] of the vessel in which he sails may be endangered by overloading it upon one side, is desirous of carrying the small weight of his reasons to that which may preserve its equipoise.

ENDNOTES

Part Two: Historical Context

1. Peter Jones, *The French Revolution, 1787–1804* (New York: Longman, 2010), 30.

2. Georges Lefebvre, *The Great Fear of 1789: Rural Panic in Revolutionary France* (New York: Schocken Books, 1989), 60ff.

3. François Buzot in Georges Lefebvre, *The Coming of the French Revolution, 1789* (Princeton, N.J.: Princeton University Press, 1971), 166.

4. Robert Blackman, "What Was 'Absolute' about the 'Absolute Veto'? Ideas of National Sovereignty and Royal Power in September 1789," *Proceedings of the Western Society for French History* 32 (2004), http://hdl.handle.net/2027/spo.0642292.0032.008 (accessed February 26, 2014).

5. Paris (France) Châtelet, Charles Chabroud, and France Assemblée Nationale Constituante (1789–1791), *Procédure criminelle instruite au Châtelet de Paris: Sur la dénonciation des faits arrivés à Versailles dans la journée du 6 octobre 1789* (Paris: Baudouin, Imprimeur de l'Assemblée Nationale, 1790).

6. Jeremy D. Popkin, *A Short History of the French Revolution* (Boston: Prentice Hall, 2010), 49.

7. See for example the historiography in Gary Kates, *The French Revolution: Recent Debates and New Controversies* (New York: Routledge, 1998).

8. C. L. James, *History of the French Revolution* (A. Isaak, Jr., 1902), 106.

9. Timothy Tackett, *Becoming a Revolutionary: The Deputies of the French National Assembly and the Emergence of a Revolutionary Culture (1789–1790)* (University Park, PA: Pennsylvania State University Press, 2006).

10. Thomas Edward Watson, *The Story of France: From the Earliest Times to the Consulate of Napoleon Bonaparte* (New York: Macmillan, 1902), 481.

ACKNOWLEDGMENTS

This game has been in continuous development for nearly 18 years. Dozens of professors and hundreds of students have raised provocative questions, unearthed revelatory sources, and offered ingenious enhancements. This game was a collaborative endeavor of the richest kind. We particularly appreciate the guidance of the Board of the Reacting Consortium, expertly chaired by John Burney since its inception. We acknowledge the sustained work of Nicolas Proctor (Simpson College), chair of the Editorial Board of the Reacting Consortium. We also cite the important contributions of John Moser (Ashland University), Gretchen McKay (McDaniel College), Judy Walden (Simpson College), John Bailly (Florida International University), Timothy Tackett (University of California—Irvine), Paula Lazrus (St. John's University), Lisa Cox (Greenfield Community College), Nancy Reagin (Pace University), and Mark Higbee (Eastern Michigan University), among so many others whose contributions have lamentably slipped from memory. All forty-two of the roles in this version of the game are based on historical figures. We thank Eric Sears for helping with this research.

We also thank Justin Cahill, editor and creative force behind the Norton RTTP project.

In acknowledging that this game was substantially a creation of the entire Reacting community, we pay special tribute to Dana Johnson of Barnard College. Not only did she build the administrative and financial superstructure of the Reacting enterprise, she also organized scores of faculty workshops and conference presentations of the game. For her work in developing this game—and the entire Reacting enterprise—we dedicate this book to her.

CPSIA information can be obtained
at www.ICGtesting.com
Printed in the USA
LVHW012252260822
726950LV00002B/184